Work It, Girl!

101 TIPS FOR THE HIP WORKING CHICK

Wendy Burt and Erin Kindberg

Contemporary Books

Chicago   New York   San Francisco   Lisbon   London   Madrid   Mexico City
Milan   New Delhi   San Juan   Seoul   Singapore   Sydney   Toronto

Library of Congress Cataloging-in-Publication Data

Burt, Wendy.
    Work it, girl! : 101 tips for the hip working chick / Wendy Burt and Erin Kindberg.
        p.   cm.
    ISBN 0-07-140901-7 (alk. paper)
        1. Women in the professions.   2. Women—Psychology.   3. Women—Life
    skills guides.   I. Kindberg, Erin.   II. Title.

    HD6054.B87   2003
    650.1'082—dc21   2003046008

1 2 3 4 5 6 7 8 9 0   DOC/DOC   2 1 0 9 8 7 6 5 4 3

ISBN 0-07-140901-7

Interior design by Nick Panos

McGraw-Hill books are available at special quantity discounts to use as premiums and sales promotions, or for use in corporate training programs. For more information, please write to the Director of Special Sales, Professional Publishing, McGraw-Hill, Two Penn Plaza, New York, NY 10121-2298. Or contact your local bookstore.

This book is printed on acid-free paper.

This book is dedicated to:
* Our wonderful agent, Deidre, and the hip working chicks at McGraw-Hill.
* Mom and Dad, who have ALWAYS encouraged me.
* The Accountability Group for surviving my regular gab sessions.
* and Aaron, Moe, and Goodie, who keep me company while I write.

Love, Wendy

Special thanks to:
* Deidre Knight and the Knight Agency, along with Denise Betts at McGraw-Hill. Without you, ladies, this book would not have been possible.
* The Nampa Kindberg clan, for the endless supply of dinners, beer, and laughs during the time I spent in Idaho working on this book. Thanks for a great year!
* My pal Kim Ketterlin, for listening to me yap.
* Mom, Mike, Lee, and Christine for their encouragement.
* . . . and to Adam, of course!

Love, Erin

CONTENTS

Introduction

More women work full-time than ever before in history. From waitresses to window washers, accountants to zoo administrators, women comprise nearly 50 percent of today's workforce. What's more, working chicks can be found in virtually all industries, holding traditional "men's jobs" like firefighter, secret service agent, and mechanic (we're still waiting on that female president, though), proving that there is no job for which a women is not qualified!

Whatever our personal history, we working women hold common bonds that make us strive to get more from our jobs. We expect and demand better pay, more fun, increased challenges, mental stimulation, physical movement, and more r-e-s-p-e-c-t—and we're getting it. That said, there are times when we need to renew our enthusiasm and motivation, when we need help getting better organized and tips for being more productive, and when we just need to be reminded to take a deep breath and have fun.

The book you're holding offers 101 tips, suggestions, and solutions to make your everyday work-related life easier, more fun, and fabulous. From dealing with an inconsiderate coworker and asking for a raise to making your commute more enjoyable and getting a workout on the job, *Work It, Girl!* can help motivate and inspire by teaching you how to take control—and responsibility—for your own happiness.

We've combined tips for hard-boiled career chicks on the fast track as well as regular gals struggling to enjoy their job while making a living. Dana the Dishwasher and Cindy the CEO have plenty in common: they both deal with work-related stress and hassles, from overtime to balancing family pressures to burnout. Chapters on organizing your Day-Timer, coping with insomnia, and getting through a flu bug can apply to all women regardless of whether they sign the paychecks from a corner office or work on the factory line that prints them.

Who needs this book, besides you? A departing employee. Your husband's boss. Your administrative assistant. Your sister's neighbor who hasn't had a raise in fifteen years. Your kid's teacher. The woman at the bakery who is red-faced and flustered every day and isn't afraid to let everyone know it. You get the idea.

Dealing with a bevy of typical workplace issues, including choosing a day-care provider, negotiating a raise with a tough boss, fighting discrimination, and maintaining your car in order to avoid commuting emergencies, you're likely to find answers to your own concerns within these pages. And since you're a busy woman, we'll spare you the stuffy career "expert advice" that insists that your job must be all-consuming and top priority, and that you must conduct yourself with the utmost professionalism if you are to succeed. Nobody says you can't have fun *and* do your job well!

How did we come up with this stuff, you ask? Simple—we're both graduates of the working woman's school commonly known as *life*. You name it, and between the two of us we've done it, whether it's slinging hash in a greasy spoon diner, scrubbing toilets to get through college, jetting off first-class to NYC on business, serving as a muffin company CEO, answering phones, writing computer manuals, or swinging around a pole in a G-string (hey, it was only for one day, and we really needed the money!).

Long gone are the days of dreading the sound of the alarm clock. With this book, you'll have the tools you need to create a work environment that you look forward to because you've addressed the problems head-on, and it will get you brainstorming on ways to learn to love—not leave—your current job.

While we're all striving toward maximum job satisfaction, remember there's always room for improvement. Be it age, education, level of interest, or need to work, not all working women are created equal when it comes to negotiating a signing bonus, writing a formal cover letter or résumé, or making the most of their company's 401(k) matching funds policy. Ditto with breaking up arguments at work, rallying coworkers, or getting a coffee stain out of your favorite white blouse. While this book can't substitute for instincts, education, or innate skills, it *will* give you fun, creative solutions to 101 work-related conundrums. The rest is up to you. Now, get out there and Work It, Girl!

—Erin and Wendy

P.S. If you like this book, you'll want to check out our first book, *Oh, Solo Mia! The Hip Chick's Guide to Fun for One*, offering 101 ideas for women to have fun solo. From parasailing and wine tastings to volunteering in your community, *Oh, Solo Mia!* makes a great gift for any woman who could use more fun in her life without the need to be accompanied by a partner, friend, or family member.

1

The Breakfast of Champions

Get your U.S. RDA to start your day right.

*"I have a simple philosophy. Fill what's empty.
Empty what's full. And scratch where it itches."*
—Alice Roosevelt Longworth

Remember when your mother used to tell you that breakfast was the most important meal of the day? With the exception of power lunches that help you move up the chain of command, she was right.

Getting the nutrients you need to energize your body for a busy morning is tough enough. But factor in the days you skip lunch, are dieting to fit into your little black dress for Saturday night, or snarf down a Big Mac because you're starving and it's cheap, and you have a body that needs fueling for a morning *and* afternoon.

So how does a girl of your limited cooking prowess eat a sensible meal without hiring a live-in chef? Think simple proteins and carbs.

You can boil water, right? Make up two hard-boiled eggs the night before, let them cool, peel them under water, then place them in a baggy for the morning commute.

Lean sandwich meat like ham or turkey can also make for a quick fuel-up on the go. Hey—no one says you can't eat "lunch" food for breakfast.

Ditto with tuna on toast, hummus on crackers, or a garbanzo bean omelet with low-fat shredded cheese and your favorite veggies.

Whole-grain toaster waffles with jam are easy to make and take—but grab a towel if you're not eating in your pajamas. As a general rule, whenever possible, eat *before* you change into your clothes for the day.

Reduced-fat peanut butter is always a good protein source and can easily be spread on whatever you have lying around: English muffins, crackers, apples, bananas, or melba toast.

Bagels and cream cheese are great for the girl on the go because they're nutritious, delicious, and relatively clean (unless you're the type that has cream cheese oozing out the sides).

Cottage cheese and fruit—such as canned mandarin oranges—is always energizing, as is yogurt over fruit cocktail.

As the name implies, "instant" oatmeal is fast. It's also nutritious—especially if it's topped with fresh fruit and wheat germ.

There are also plenty of cereals on the market that can provide you with many of the vitamins and minerals your body needs to kick some serious butt at the office without the comedown that caffeine leaves. Look for cereals that are high in fiber, carbs, vitamins, and minerals, but low in fat. Granola is a good bet if it's low-fat, with or without raisins. It's also a great midmorning snack—even without milk.

Your best bet is to think ahead. Set your coffee pot to perk as you get out of bed. Take your shower the night before so you're not rushing out the door with no breakfast due to time constraints. Set out your vitamins for the week in a pill box organizer.

If you can plan, purchase, and prepare in advance, your morning will most likely leave you feeling energized—not depleted. Desperate times call for desperate measures—and that little black dress isn't getting any bigger.

What to Look For

Buy quick-to-eat cereals and cereal bars that are high in whole grains or whole wheat, but avoid those that list sugar as the first ingredient.

Fun Factoid

In rural homes in the nineteenth century, apple and other fruit pie was a common item served for breakfast, considered a good hearty beginning for a hard day's work. (**Source:** foodreference.com)

2

Shower Serenade

You don't have time for a three-minute conditioner.

Are you the type of gal who wakes up without an alarm clock and breezes through her morning ritual, arriving to work fresh faced and three minutes early to boot? If so, skip ahead . . . this chapter's for the punctuality-challenged chick who rousts herself from bed after slapping the snooze button three times and chugs coffee while still practically comatose, finally arriving at work wearing one blue shoe and one black shoe.

Some blissful days, you can skip that shower and feel presentable enough to go out in public. Just throw on a little deodorant, wash that face, and your bod is a presentable enough palette to throw some clothes on. But if anything less than one shower a day leaves you feeling like a greasy bohemian who lives in a van, do yourself and the rest of the world a favor and bathe already—but do it in record time.

You can shave shower time down to two minutes flat, even *with* a hair washing. How? With an egg timer to keep you on the ball and products that do double duty, that's how! A "wet chic" hairdo doesn't hurt, either.

First, take your kitchen timer into the bathroom with you and set it to two minutes. Not only will it keep you on a supertight grooming schedule, but the very act of setting it signals your brain by saying, "Hey, we're in a hurry. Get lathered and get going!" It may also help spare you from the grooming routine dillydallies: you know, when you go to tackle the stinky parts and soon find yourself saying, "Hmmm, sandal season's on the way . . . I think I'll scrub the barnacles off my feet while my deep conditioner soaks into my tresses . . ." When that bell dings, you're done!

The other key, besides tackling tasks like shaving and deep conditioning the night before? Double duty products! Why clean *and* moisturize *and* shampoo *and* condition with four different goos when you could just clean/moisturize *and* shampoo/condition? Thanks to some savvy product combinations and the benefits of living in the twenty-first century with a drugstore on every corner, you have nothing short of a mountain of products boasting effective leave-in conditioners available to you. Now if some smart company would create a lathery total body miracle that cleans, conditions, and dries leaving big bouncy curls that last all day (and erases cellulite plus makes your feet smell like gardenia blooms after a ten-hour day, since we're dreaming), we'd all be in business.

The other benefit of the two-minute shower, besides an abbreviated primp time? Better skin! Beauty experts swear that slathering lotion on to cure dry skin is only half the equation: shorter, cooler showers help your skin retain more moisture in the first place.

Get the accompanying "no time to do my hair" hairdo and you're all set. Smart chicks pick styles that looked pulled together and smart in a few minutes flat (not to be confused with the "trailer park trash" greasy brown ponytail look, which is also ready in no time at all). Cornrows, French twists, super short, and spiky are all fabulous, super-quick 'dos. Ask your stylist for advice on an easy-to-style cut.

Unless your job is one that has you spinning around a pole in thigh-high boots and pasties, leave the fifty-minute mousse/blow/tease/set/spray routine to trophy wives.

3

Makeup or Break-up

Master the sixty-second makeup job.

If you wake up looking more like Bo Diddly than Bo Derek, you'll want to master the sixty-second makeup job. (*Not* to be confused with the sixty-*minute* makeup job seen in many major metropolitan areas.)

Its basic premise is this: if you were stranded on a desert island and could only take two cosmetics, what would they be? (Nowadays, sunscreen is a given, so let's discount that as a cosmetic for argument's sake.) Of course, we'll have to assume that you're not alone on the island, or you wouldn't care—save for the day you're rescued and blanketed with a swarm of media people.

So let's say you've chosen mascara and blush. Great! Now you know where to focus your sixty seconds. If you chose lipstick or lip gloss as one of your two items, even better! Unlike mascara, lipstick and gloss are easily applied at a stoplight or standstill with no mirror.

The lipstick technique itself is not to be taken lightly, as the multi-generational secret has been handed down from grandmothers to mothers to daughters for decades. (Why do you think they make those tiny purses that fit nothing more than a tube of lipstick and an o.b. tampon?)

There *is* another alternative to performing the sixty-second makeup job at home—performing the sixty-second makeup job at work! This could mean any number of things: the quick application in the parking lot, the spruce-up in the restroom on your first coffee break, or the "primp-on-the-pot" mad dash to the bathroom in the first ten minutes of your workday.

Yes, there is such a thing as an "on-the-road application," but we don't recommend it and neither does the highway patrol. Drawing on eyebrows at fifty-five miles per hour is a disaster waiting to happen in more ways than one. If you must wear makeup, better to take the extra sixty seconds at home—and perhaps the tardiness tongue-lashing from your boss—to increase your chances of making it through another day of high-speed traffic.

There are a few tricks to make the most of your morning makeup minute:

* Keep the essentials in a small zippered pouch. It'll not only help you find everything in a pinch, but it's much easier to throw into your briefcase for touch-ups later in the day. Plus, if your open compact breaks into a thousand pieces, it will remain in the pouch (assuming you remember to keep it zippered!).
* Use your time wisely. Good times to apply makeup? While the iron warms up. While your computer boots up. While your car warms up. (Do you see a pattern here?)
* Opt for two-in-one makeup whenever possible—a lipstick that also serves as a blush, a blush/eye shadow combo, or a moisturizing/SPF concealer that serves multiple purposes but only requires one application.

Whatever option you choose for your quick makeup job—the house, the commute, the office—just remember that haste makes waste. You may want to check your face right before you head into that big staff meeting: lip liner and brow pencil feel exactly the same when you're running late.

4

Suit Yourself

Have a plan for when every blouse you own is wrinkled.

"Clothes never shut up."
—Susan Brownmiller

Your worst nightmare has come true! (No, chocolate hasn't been found to be detrimental to your health.) You got carried away at last night's Margarita and Mexican Food Fiesta, fell asleep on the couch, and woke up way too late. Your intentions of waking up early to a power breakfast, leisurely ironing your best outfit, and pounding out a five-mile run to really get those neurons firing are dashed!

Fear not, savvy career chick! You have an emergency plan for just such an occasion . . . don't you? If not, plan ahead today for such clothing crises tomorrow!

When it comes to smart and stress-free dressing for your job, 99 percent of clothing crises can be avoided by simply planning ahead. Rather than throwing clothes in the dryer and forgetting about them, be sure to remove items as soon as the buzzer sounds. Using the appropriate setting helps, too, since most "medium" dryer settings include a ten-minute cooldown that helps cut wrinkles. With so many fabric options available, choose carefree blends like Tencel, polyester blends, and knit tops and slacks. Forget high-maintenance fabrics like dry-clean-only rayon and wrinkle-prone linens. Also, take just thirty minutes on Sunday to plan your wardrobe for the week, so you're not rushing around searching for something to wear at the last minute.

Still, what do you do when everything you own is a wrinkled mess? Grab the first halfway presentable outfit and do a quick assessment: are we talking "linen pants balled up at the bottom of the laundry basket and forgotten about" wrinkled, or minor-league rumpled? Let's hope it's the latter. Spray the offending shirt and/or pants with salvation in a squirt bottle, a.k.a. spray wrinkle remover (check the laundry soap aisle of your local store).

If ready-made spray wrinkle remover is too spendy, don't fret. Make your own by mixing one part generic fabric softener with three parts water, and keep it in a spray bottle in your closet. Careful, though—some dry-clean-only items are unforgiving when spritzed with anything water based.

Still feeling sloppy, even after the spray wrinkle remover? Take wrinkle assault to the next level: the dryer. Throw those togs in, and when you get out of the shower, viola—ready-to-wear and (relatively) wrinkle-free clothing! Practically any pair of pants or cotton shirt will snap to attention in a hurry when placed in the dryer. Just remember to choose the warm setting over high, and pull your clothes out after ten minutes, or risk turning your favorite rayon slacks into a pair of bun-hugging high-waters.

Still no good? Don't panic! Time to break out your emergency outfit, which you smartly should have set aside *before* you need it. This is the outfit that's ready to throw on when you need to look good in sixty seconds flat, and should include a pre-ironed top, slacks, and jacket with an unopened package of nylons. Stick this outfit in the coat closet so you save it for a truly needy occasion, rather than a momentary fit of laziness.

And next time, be sure to hang your clothes up as soon as the dryer goes off!

Women in History

Fabric stain deterrent Scotchgard was created by inventor Patsy Sherman back in 1956. Next time your ice cream cone goes "kerplop" on your sofa cushion and you're able to wipe it up in a jiff, you likely have Patsy's fabulous fabric treatment to thank.

5

Ladies, Start Your Engines

Maintain a vehicle you can count on.

"If you can read this, I can slam on my brakes and sue you."
—Bumper sticker

Think the worst part of working in winter is the sprint from the warmth of your down comforter to the cool bathroom tile? Think again! Nothing sends chills up your nylon-clad gams like the icy blast from the dashboard of a neglected car. Unlike hereditary cellulite, however, there are solutions to your problem.

First and foremost, you must learn to take care of your car. Sure, there are plenty of people to take care of it when it breaks, but why wait until it's too late? If you take preventive measures, you're bound to feel safer, save money, and keep your car for longer.

The number one rule in car ownership is similar to body ownership: get your checkups. Every three thousand miles you should plan to take your car in for an oil change. Don't worry if you can't remember what your mileage was last time you stopped in. Most places will give you a small sticker for your windshield that will remind you when to come back. Although a typical oil change costs about $25 to $35, you'll probably be able to find coupons in your local paper for deals like "$10 off" or "$14.95 special"—especially if you're in a city where there's lots of competition.

Some places will also check your fluids, your tire pressure, your fil-ters, etc. for free. Ask ahead of time (by calling) so you know which auto shop will give you the most bang for your buck. You may want to check with your local Better Business Bureau to make sure your choice of shops is trustworthy and has a good reputation with no unresolved complaints.

Once you trust your mechanic, listen to his advice. Sure, there's a chance he's trying to bilk you for more money, but that's why you did your research, right? Instead, get a list of any recommended repairs and get a second opinion if necessary. Also, feel free to ask questions and have him show you (and explain) why you need new tires or other work.

Even the best-kept car is susceptible to problems; however, the important thing is to be prepared. Obviously, carrying a cell phone is ideal, but there are plenty of times that it may not work—or it may take time for help to arrive. As a backup, have an emergency kit in your car. Be sure to include a flashlight, warm blankets, layered cloth-ing, some bottled water and nonperishable food, jumper cables, an orange and white flag or cloth to tie to your antenna, a portable radio, batteries, matches, and candles.

If you treat your car right, you'll most likely have a safe, cozy vehi-cle for your daily commute. You'll be especially glad you've taken care of your "baby" on those cold, snowy days when you would otherwise need to wrap your fingers around a scorching hot latte just to retain circulation.

Although you may want to maximize your heat production by let-ting your car warm up, be careful not to overheat your vehicle. You'll also need to be aware of any city ordinances that prohibit you from idling for more than ten minutes. No one wants to save all that money on fixing her car only to have to spend it on a ticket.

Speaking of cars . . .

Need a fix of fixing something? Check out *Auto Repair for Dummies* by Deanna Schlar and learn to do some minor repairs yourself!

Fun Factoid

Mary Anderson invented the windshield wiper. Anderson noticed that streetcar drivers had to open the windows of their cars when it rained in order to see. As a solution she invented the windshield wiper in 1903. She was issued a patent in 1905. The wipers were standard equipment on all American cars by 1916.

6

Backroad Warrior

Take a new route each day to combat commute boredom.

"The cure for boredom is curiosity. There is no cure for curiosity."
—Ellen Parr

Head south on the interstate. Whiz past the peeling "Got Milk?" billboard for the umpteenth time. Idle at the predictably long stoplight. Is your commute like a terminally boring movie stuck on repeat five days a week?

It doesn't have to be! Shake things up by ditching your old route to the office and launching an expedition through unexplored side streets and back alleys of your town. Tons of time-saving shortcuts are just waiting to be tunneled out next time you're heading to work.

Don't think something as simple as a new route can freshen your outlook? Whoa, there, Negative Nellie! Who knows what exciting consignment boutiques, doughnut shops, funky junk shops, and other urban gems exist along the new route. Plus, banishing even one iota of sameness may help lend a fresh perspective to your day and give you a new view over the dashboard horizon. As a bonus, you may shave five or more minutes off your arrival time by taking a less predictable route than the rest of the commuters.

Start by getting a city map. You may think you know the best, and therefore only, way to work, but you may be surprised. Rip the city map out of the phone book, or buy one at your next gas pit stop. Pretend you're brand new to the city and chart an alternate course to work. Don't be shy about straying off the highway and accessing other thoroughfares that may get you there tons quicker, even factoring in stoplights. While the rest of those commuter chumps languish in stop-and-go traffic on the highway, you could be pulling into your parking space five minutes early and smiling smugly!

Mapquest.com and many other Internet sites offer instant driving directions and printable maps perfect for charting your course. These sites give instant directions to just about anywhere, simply by entering your house as Point A and the office as Point B. The route a site suggests may have you saying to yourself, "I didn't know Peachtree Boulevard went south all the way to Overland. That gets me halfway to work in nothing flat!"

Or, call in a professional—dial your local commuter or public transportation office for suggested routes. These sources will be happy to give you the dirt on construction projects that could detour your new route into a dead end.

Still bored? Switch cars with your hubby or significant other for the heck of it. Maybe getting stuck with your crappy, hole-in-the-muffler heap of a car will offer a rattly reminder that he promised to fix it for you. And you'll get to mow over any unsuspecting road ragers who challenge you while you tool along the tollway in his shiny new SUV!

Just remember any parking passes or security badges that you'll need before you go ripping out of the driveway. Banishing boredom is good, but getting stuck in his car at the parking meter without your ever-present roll of quarters in the ashtray is a bummer.

7

Bookworm in the Fast Lane

Enjoy great audiotapes on your commute.

"This book fills a much-needed gap."
—Moses Hadas

Have you ever been stuck in traffic and thought, "This is great! I hope this line doesn't clear for a while. I'm enjoying this."

No? Well you may be surprised to learn that some people do feel this way. No, they're not sadomasochists and there's no New Age meditation ritual involved, and it's something that almost anyone can do. So what is it? Listen to books on tape!

The possibilities are endless, as you can see when you realize that (1) you love to read, (2) you hate wasting time, and (3) you never have enough time to read.

Listening to books on tape is a great way for today's commuter (by car, bus, train, or subway) to lower her blood pressure before or after a long day of stress. Of course, there are rules against driving with headphones—so you'll need to make sure your tape player is working in your car.

There are *no* rules, however, on what type of audiocassette you can choose.

Feeling sexy because you're going to see the vending machine guy today? Why not pop in some erotic romance novel and imagine Pepsi

Pants in the role of the leading male? (Yes, that makes you the heroine . . .)

Bored with the usual office hubbub of "Who used the last mustard?" Pop in a *real* mystery with political scandal, intrigue, and murder.

Waxing nostalgic? Search out a historical epoch or "stand by me" novel that'll leave you laughing and crying for the week's commute.

Before you know it you'll be whipping through cassettes faster than you can wave in three lines of cars (much to the dismay of the truck behind you). You'll be skipping out early just to get to your car and sitting in your driveway while you learn who really fathered Catherine's sister's baby before going off to war.

Of course, books on tape don't grow on trees. They can, however, be found for free. Most libraries now carry a vast selection of audiocassettes, and some libraries will even order a book if it's requested enough.

You'll just have to disguise your voice when you call to request *Lady Chatterley's Lover* for the sixteenth time.

Good Choices on Audiocassette

* Like mysteries? Check out any of Sue Grafton's novels—beginning with *A Is for Alibi* and ending in *Q Is for Quarry*.
* Enjoy motivational tapes to get you off your duff? Listen to Tony Robbins and you'll be crossing off your to-do list in no time.
* Need some laughs? Listen to anything by David Sedaris, like *Me Talk Pretty One Day*.
* Bored with your own life's lack of romance? Listen to a Sidney Sheldon or Jacqueline Suzanne book on tape and your windows will be steaming in no time!
* Is horror your thing? Check out a Dean Koontz or Stephen King thriller and you'll be crying for your mama!

8

Beauty School Dropout

Try these safe on-the-road beauty tips.

In a perfect world, you'd wake up without an alarm clock, spend a leisurely hour over coffee in fuzzy slippers with the paper, then shuffle into your cavernous marble bathroom. You'd begin with your skuzzy self and emerge a lotioned, powdered, and primped career woman, supremely ready to conquer Wall Street (or the checkout line at Walgreen's, depending on where you work).

Unfortunately, a real morning for many of us looks more like a puffy-eyed bolt from bed, a quick swig of lukewarm coffee savored between rousing the kids and letting the dog out to pee. Primp? Oh, please! You'd be lucky to brush your teeth and find two socks that match.

Lucky for you, you have a long commute. It's the perfect opportunity to give your head a little "rearview mirror redux." You don't want to pull into the parking lot and spill out of the sedan looking like a sleep-deprived sea hag! With a little advance planning, you can save time and brain damage by prettying up on the way to work.

Your fast lane froufrouing will be better served with a kit for just that purpose. As any highway patrol officer would tell you, forget rummaging through your purse at eighty miles an hour and save primping for the stoplight. Everything you need should be within reach and minimally messy, such as:

* **Wet/dry base:** Sort of a gooey powder, it gives you a finished look without all that spreading and sponging fuss.
* **Lipstick without liner:** Put your Angelina Jolie aspirations aside and pick a sheer shade that doesn't require total precision on your part. Skip the lip liner altogether. Lip liner combined with a sudden green light will have you either looking like your shaky Great-aunt Gladys or merging onto a median, making the perfect pout a moot point.
* **Scrunchies, clips, and hair bands:** Don't think fluffing and spraying's gonna hide that pillow-induced cowlick on the back of your head. (You can't see it, but trust us, it's there!) If it's long, pull it back and be done with it. Leave a hair band or two on your gearshift, just in case. If it's short, get creative with hair accessories. Forget hair spray in the car, since it's murder on the interior.
* **Blush and eye shadow:** These are two-handers. Save them for the bathroom once you arrive, or go without. Why? Refer to the Great-aunt Gladys comment above.
* **Mascara:** Unless your name happens to be Elizabeth Arden, you probably need a coat or two of basic black mascara to avoid the beady little rat eyes look. Supposedly, French women swear that thick black mascara coupled with bright red lipstick is a surefire way to avoid looking sleep deprived.

Fun Factoid

With a commute of thirty-nine minutes, New Yorkers spend about an entire day more in their cars each year than workers in Chicago, who have a thirty-three-minute average commute. The runners-up for longest commute? San Francisco, Oakland, and Newark.

9

The Best Laid Plans

Organize your Day-Timer to save time, money,
and your career.

> *"It's the good girls who keep the diaries;
> the bad girls never have the time."*
> **—Tallulah Bankhead**

If you've ever bought a belated birthday card, you could probably use a little help organizing your Day-Timer. If you never mailed that belated birthday card, you probably need a lot of help.

And forgetting birthday cards probably doesn't affect your career. What about those missed appointments or staff meetings?

Good news. Organizing your Day-Timer can not only help your career, but your relationships, self-esteem, motivation, and even finances! Just follow these simple tips and you're on your way to a more efficient lifestyle.

If you don't already have a Day-Timer, now is the time to buy one. This doesn't mean spending hundreds on some fancy Italian leather contraption. In fact, many thrift stores will sell the leather case for as little as one to five dollars. Then you can head to your local office supply store and buy the insert pages that fit your specific needs.

Start with the basics: a daily planner packet typically includes one to two pages per day with a by-hour time block as well as a one-page monthly calendar. You may also want to buy an address section and several folders for coupons, stamps, greeting cards, and receipts. If you need an expense sheet, buy one that's divided by month or expenses (mileage, meals, hotels, food, etc.). You may want to purchase a small notepad or "to-do" sheet that tucks in the front flap.

Fill in all your important events: birthdays, anniversaries, special events, etc. Then go back and add things you need to do to prepare for such events. For example, if your mother's birthday is August 16, write "buy Mom's card" on August 12 and "call Mom" on her actual birthday. Ditto with "make hotel reservations" months before a big trip.

Your best bet for fighting procrastination is to be prepared. Always carry stamps and a few blank cards that can double for birthday and thank-you emergencies. It's always helpful to write out thank-you cards right after a meeting or the receipt of a gift or service to ensure you won't forget (and to show a prompt courtesy).

Keeping coupons for food, products, and services is a sure way to save money. How many times have you meant to bring your coupon only to end up paying full price?

Keeping receipts handy can help with reimbursement for work. They also allow for a quick exchange when you later realize you bought the wrong size or brand and don't have time to go home for the receipt again.

When you make a daily to-do list, cross off items as you accomplish them. At the end of the day, just move any unaccomplished goals to the next page.

Whenever you have an important meeting, make a note on the day before to call and confirm your appointment to avoid wasting time and travel expenses. Whenever possible, choose one day a week to make all your phone calls to save on costly interruptions. Ditto with grouping errands together. Keep a running grocery list on your notepad to avoid return trips and last-minute (more expensive!) purchases. Write in refill prescription dates a week or two before you run out to avoid missing any pills when it's too late to get a refill.

Although planning sometimes seems like more trouble than it's worth, it will actually save you time, money—and maybe some embarrassment. Besides, remembering Aunt Edna's birthday might keep her from forgetting yours.

10

Relocating for a New Job

Check out your new environment before you move.

> *"There is always room at the top."*
> —**Daniel Webster**

Your day has finally arrived! After years of schlepping, copying, working late, and otherwise paying your dues, you've landed a fabulous new job. Here's the catch: the new job is in another city.

Whether scoping out opportunities on your own or moving within the same company, work-related relocations are at an all-time high. No matter what industry you're in, there's a chance that climbing the ladder of success may mean stepping off the rung you're on into a whole new city.

How do you handle such a major move? With the same savvy and work finesse that landed you the new job in the first place, of course.

If you've already accepted the position, the time is now to find out how your company will handle the move. Does the company offer to pay moving expenses, or are you on your own? Don't be shy about asking specifics: are you to pack your own stuff and drive a truck across the country, or is your company calling in professional movers to pack and transport you? Also, you'll most likely be breaking a lease or selling your home to make the move happen. Find out if you'll be reimbursed for the cost of lease penalties or mortgage payments while your house is vacant.

Once it's a done deal, it's time to get organized. Get online and do a cost-of-living comparison between your current and future cities for a financial snapshot of the future. This information helps you to know what sort of lifestyle your new city will support. That way, you'll know to brace yourself before moving from a $500-a-month rental house in Podunk to a $1,900 Bay-area studio apartment (not to mention the wardrobe adjustment such a move would require . . .). Call your car insurance agent to see how rates change as well. Some rates as much as double for identical coverage when moving from rural to urban areas.

While you're at it, check out the slew of relocation sites online. Any city of commerce worth its salt will have an official website with relocation information. For a small fee, you can likely order an official relocation packet, filled with maps, neighborhood information, and other stuff to start with. If you don't know your new city from a hole in the ground—and don't want to end up renting a place in the worst neighborhood in town—this is helpful info. Here's an unofficial rule of thumb when getting to know a new city: start researching areas close to a city's university district—these are usually fresh, vibrant communities.

Getting excited yet? Consider splurging on a "go see" visit to your new city. (Hey, maybe that's reimbursable too!) Call ahead to set up time with a Realtor or apartment finding service, and plan on a marathon day or two of looking at potential new homes, getting to know new routes around town, and scoping out your new favorite pizza joint. Bring a camera to snap pictures of potential new homes so you can visualize where your couch will go.

While you're there, consider opening a checking account to get things rolling. Paying initial utility deposits and picking up necessities will go much more smoothly with a local checking account. Conversely, switch your old account back home to a bank with countrywide branches, if you're choosy about your banking.

Lastly, go out on a high note with the old gang, and resist the urge to burn bridges if you've had a bad experience. While it's likely the new job will be fabulous and you'll never be back, there are no guarantees a job will work out. It would be nice to know that if the fast track moves a little too rapidly for you and you find yourself missing that $500 Podunk house, the option exists to come back and resume your old job.

Tips for Relocating

Check out these websites for more info on relocating to a new city:

- homefair.com
- monstermoving.com

11

ſubway ſtorieſ

Catch up on your reading and enjoy the ride.

"The last of the human freedoms—to choose one's attitude in any given set of circumstances, to choose one's own way."
—Viktor Frankl

Not that the subway is boring. On the contrary; there are generally hundreds of new faces to study even on your daily route. Problem is, not everyone likes to be looked at. In fact, you may stare at that green-haired guy with the eyebrow barbell a second too long before he comes over to ask you (A) what you're staring at, or (B) for your phone number. Either way, it would be nice to have a distraction.

If you're the type of gal who just can't learn enough, use your commute to catch up on the pile of trade or business magazines you've been saving for a rainy day. From *BusinessWeek* to *Working Woman*, there's something for every taste—and every career. You'll have the latest up-to-date information on what's happening in your industry, and the facts and figures may be just enough to get you that promotion.

For example, slip an article about your competition into your boss's "to-do" box with a note about how your company can get ahead. Or bring some stats to your next marketing meeting with ideas on how to bring your company into the Fortune 500 this year.

There are also plenty of self-help career, business, and social books that can help catapult your career into the fast lane. (After all, you're reading *this* book, aren't you?) What about something on speed reading, self-confidence, or networking? The Dummies series is always a great place to start.

If you'd rather escape a stressful day (read: "leave your work at work"), opt instead for a book to help your personal life. Perhaps something on relationships, investing, paying down credit card debt, or even how to cook gourmet for one.

If you just can't bear the thought of practical reading, opt for some fiction. There are plenty of bestsellers to choose from, or you could always go with an old standby you read when you were in college.

If the novel of choice is just too embarrassing to be seen in public (e.g., Danielle Steel's *Irresistible Forces*), there's always the old "bait and switch" move: a well-placed impressive novel, such as *War and Peace*, with its pages carefully cut out and stuffed full of your naughty novel. The move is a bit sneaky, but will not only protect your ego but perhaps also impress that hot college English professor sitting across from you. Just be sure you've already read at least the Cliffs Notes of the outside book in case the questions start flying.

᭯ Speaking of books . . .

Check out some of the books from the Dummies series:
- *Investing for Dummies* by Eric Tyson
- *Home Buying for Dummies* by Eric Tyson and Ray Brown
- *Personal Finance for Dummies* by Eric Tyson
- *Wine for Dummies* by Ed McCarthy and Mary Ewing-Mulligan
- *Grant Writing for Dummies* by Beverly A. Browning
- *Digital Photography All-in-One Desk Reference for Dummies* by David D. Busch

- *Golf for Dummies* by Gary McCord
- *Starting an eBay Business for Dummies* by Marsha Collier
- *Guitar for Dummies* by Mark Phillips
- *Sewing for Dummies* by Janice S. Saunders
- *Weight Training for Dummies* by Liz Neporent and Suzanne Schlosberg

12

Clear the Deck ... or Is That Desk?

Make your life easier with these desk organizing strategies.

> "Better keep yourself clean and bright; you are the window
> through which you must see the world."
> —George Bernard Shaw

If you're like most office dwellers, your workstation is your world five days a week. While most of us get the point in having a comfy and functional home, some working girls don't see that having a comfy, organized workstation can be a huge boon.

Stacks of files, papers left unfiled, yesterday's coffee mug, and a picture of the ex-boyfriend may not seem like a big deal ... until you consider what they're telling your subconscious. All that half-done work and those reminders of yesterday's news can clog up your consciousness, rather than making space in the universe for new stuff (men included!).

So, clear the deck already! But first, a few tips are in order to ensure you don't simply cram everything into the top drawer of your desk.

If you have a messy desk, chances are you're a "piler" who leaves stuff out in stacks in the hopes of getting to it tomorrow. Trouble is, all those stacks clutter up your work space, and probably don't get done any faster by languishing in your in box. Try the holding file technique:

take three files and label them "Important: Act Now!" "Review by Friday," and "Low Priority." When hot projects and emergencies come across your desk, stick them in the "Important" file, to be acted on immediately. Have a task that you can put off a few days? The paper goes in the Friday file, which you pull out by week's end and conclude by either completing, filing in its permanent place, shredding, or bouncing to the Low Priority file.

The trick is to remember to tackle the Friday file by Friday. Write yourself a reminder to make Friday's file a priority, otherwise important tasks may be forgotten. The Low Priority file is just as it sounds: stick FYI memos, flyers for upcoming classes, and the company softball schedule inside, to be pulled out during a slow day.

Not sure about the holding file technique? Make life even easier by having just one file, marked "Incoming." Paperclip the important stuff together with a sticky note that reads "Do this now!" and put the bundle at the top of the file. When a task is done, take it out of the file. Simple as that! Instead of rifling through your dusty in box muttering, "OK, now where is that memo about that report that's due? Hmmm . . . ," just reach in your drawer and look in your Incoming file. Keeping one single file eliminates the mystery of where your stuff is.

Now that your desk is cleared, put some stuff on it to help make your workday more productive and happier. Plop a cute pencil cup and fat pad of notepaper next to your computer, if you're a notesy kind of person. Just seeing that paper and colorful bouquet of markers says, "Hey, use us to write down all those fabulous ideas!" Another good desktop item is a plant to help regenerate oxygen, bring some natural beauty to counteract your fluorescent-bathed work space, and represent your blooming career . . . unless it withers, then quick—into the trash! A desktop aquarium is a pleasant, albeit high-maintenance addition. Skip having a sad, single beta fish in a tiny fishbowl and choose a few easy goldfish. (Side note: those tiny cups betas are sold in are supposed to be temporary until you can get your finny little guy to a real aquarium. How would *you* like to be held in a tiny bowl with no room to move?)

Taking just two minutes at the end of the workday to clear your desk will pay off in spades. You'll not only come in tomorrow and have a clean slate to work with, but clearing off helps signal closure of your workday and the "putting away" of work matters till tomorrow, which is great for Nervous Nellies who have a tendency to carry work-related angst around all day.

13

ʃpeaking in Tongueʃ

Learn how to say "I love my job!" in ten languages.

> *"I have a brain and a uterus, and I use both."*
> —**Congresswoman Patricia Schroeder**

We all know that speaking a language other than English (and pig latin) can help you land dates in foreign countries. But did you ever think that the skill might also help you skip a few rungs on the corporate ladder?

Depending on where you work and/or who your clients are, learning Spanish, French, Chinese, or Japanese could help your career as you offer to interpret for your boss. You may find yourself being asked to sit in on the monthly board of directors meeting after you nonchalantly point out that the company's Taiwan manufacturing branch slipped in a clause to start doubling its shipping costs. "We need someone with Sue's language skills to keep us abreast of our partnerships overseas," the chairman will explain as he passes you the phone number of his travel agent. "Pack your bags, Sue. We're going to negotiate in person."

Speaking a second language doesn't necessarily have to lead to contract interpretations. You could use your newfound skill to communicate with customers who speak English as a second language. Whether you're a customer service representative, a receptionist, a vice president, or an accountant, communicating with clients is a top priority and adapting to meet their needs is a value-added service.

When choosing a language, consider your geographic location. If you're a teacher in Tucson, chances are you're not going to have a lot of Russian-speaking kids. Ditto for the massage therapist in Maine; think French Canadian!

On the other hand, if you're a nurse in New York City, well, good luck trying to narrow it down to one language. The city's an eclectic melting pot of culture, and there are probably plenty of times you'll need to use many different languages.

You may also want to consider learning sign language. You'll probably have to rent a videotape or get a book from the library (as opposed to an audiocassette), but think of the possibilities once you do learn the skill. You could offer to sign at church, volunteer at a nearby school for the deaf, or teach sign language to other children and adults. You may not have as many opportunities to use it through work, but if someone else in your office learns with you, you sure could have a lot of fun practicing on the job!

Speaking of language cassettes ...

Check out these great audio books to learn a new language quickly:

- *Speak French (German/Italian/Spanish) with Michel Thomas* by Michel Thomas
- *Drive-In Chinese/German/Italian/Japanese/Russian/French/Spanish* by Jane Wightwick et al.
- *Just Listen 'n Learn Arabic/Chinese/French/German/Greek/Italian/ Japanese/Russian/French/Spanish*, Brian Hill, General Editor

14

Hands-Free Gossip

Catch up on calls with a headset while you're stuck in traffic.

> *"Hang up and drive."*
> **—Bumper sticker**

You've gotta love twenty-first-century technology. Living in the modern age has brought women such niceties as hair-zapping lasers, TV sets the size of a thumbnail, and cell phones that make it possible to indulge in intercontinental gossip.

Look around during any stoplight, and chances are you'll see fellow drivers using their cell phones to catch up on calls. Research suggests that of the more than 100 million folks with cell phones, 85 percent of them yap while driving. While using commute time to conduct calls makes lots of sense, yapping away and dialing a cell phone while whizzing down the freeway does not. One wrong move or split second of distraction, and you'd better hope your phone's in one piece so you can call 911.

The answer? A cell phone headset, of course! Headsets let you make calls and keep both hands on the wheel, without having to juggle the phone. If you've never used this handy contraption on your wireless and it's still sitting in the box, dig it out. Whether they're the earbud version or the wrap style, headsets feel a little like mutated Walkman headphones and make may you feel a little like you're a telephone operator. But try it a few times and you'll be hooked! Plenty of savvy cell yappers even use the hands-free option to chat while shop-ping, standing in line in stores, just about anywhere. Just ignore the initial stares you get from people who don't realize you're on the phone rather than just talking to yourself.

Plenty of wireless companies now throw in a free headset to sweeten the deal. If you're thinking of making the move to wireless, ask about hands-free options for the phones the company offers. Some of the more uptown models have all sorts of cool options, including noise-reducing microphones and super-lightweight two-ounce models.

Or, buy a nifty new headset for the phone you already have. Pop into any wireless store for a cheapie that fits the 2.5-millimeter jack that is standard on most wireless phones. There are models for fifteen bucks or less, so money's hardly an issue. To save time, simply order one online: scads of websites sell them (cellphone.com, headsets.com, headsetwholesaler.com . . . the list goes on and on). Just make sure the headset's compatible with your phone before you buy—most sell-ers don't allow returns, since subsequent users don't want ear cooties. (That must be why for long flights airlines now hand out headsets that are neatly encased in hermetically sealed plastic bags!)

While you're at it, why not put your most often placed calls on speed dial? That way your boss, best friend, or new boy toy hottie are only a few digits away from being reached, further cutting the time you have to fiddle with the phone when you really should be driving.

Just think: not juggling your cell phone leaves your hands free to do all the other stuff you usually do behind the wheel but shouldn't, whether it's touching up your Tahitian Temptation lipstick, changing CDs, or digging that last fry from the bottom of the bag. The habit of multitasking behind the wheel dies hard, indeed.

15

No Place Like Home

Take control of your day to work from home more effectively.

> "Life is like a sewer—you get out of it what you put into it."
> —**Tom Lehrer**

It could be a sick day, a holiday, or maybe just an added incentive from a company that trusts its employees and honors the parents that need to stay home with their kids. Whatever the reason, consider yourself lucky: you get to work at home today!

Before you go channel-surfing for Oprah's hot topic of the day, take note: working at home means just that—*working*.

You're still expected to produce, perform, and be professional— you've just been given the added bonus of working in your pajamas. (Don't worry, you have a few years before your company buys the video phones . . .)

Your first obstacle will be to overcome distractions, mainly television, nonwork phone calls, household chores, and interruptions from kids, partners, friends, and roommates. Working from home requires that you set boundaries. This may mean closing the door to your office, letting the answering machine pick up (or screen) calls, and putting a sign on your door that says "Work in progress. Please return or call after 5 P.M."

Granted, there may still be emergencies and things that just have to be dealt with: a crying baby, a pet that needs to go out, or a neighbor who has locked herself out of her house and needs to borrow your phone. The trick is to handle the situation quickly and effectively and get back to work.

For some, a to-do list works wonders. Breaking a larger project into smaller tasks will not only help you feel like you're getting work accomplished, but may also allow for scheduled breaks before moving on to the next item on your list.

An egg timer or alarm clock may also help you work for a scheduled amount of time while teaching small children that "Mommy will take a break when the buzzer sounds. Until then, it's quiet time."

Keeping pets busy with bones or children occupied with books, crafts, and educational videos may allow you to better focus on the work at hand without interruptions.

If you're expecting calls from clients, try to schedule your child's nap during that time or offer to call the client back "on your dime" so you have time to get a young child settled in.

If you don't have call waiting and are expecting a call, tell well-meaning friends or family members that you'll need to call them back at a later time. Don't let them pressure you into talking with phrases like "Oh, this will only take a few minutes." Politely refuse and set a time to call them back. "Joan, I'd be happy to call you back after dinner tonight. Let's say 7 P.M. Right now, I'm expecting an important call from a client that I can't miss. Thanks for understanding."

If Joan continues to call you on days that she knows you're working at home, you may want to stop dropping hints and start asking favors. "Oh, Joan. I'm so glad you called. Since Fridays are my days to work at home, I was wondering if you could watch the kids on Fridays from now on." Chances are, Joan will not only stop calling on your workdays at home, but may stop calling altogether.

16

Flextime in the Fast Lane

Jump-start your day with an audiotaped to-do list.

"Life is too short for traffic."
—Dan Bellack

Why not combine your hatred for wasting time with your love for staying organized by taking a tape recorder on your commute to work? Nothing fights traffic troubles like using your time wisely—and what better way than to make a hands-free audio to-do list!

You'll be able to tackle your daily must-dos in a stoplight brainstorming session without having to worry about looking up from your notepad to find that you've rear-ended a $75,000 Mercedes, run over your neighbor's prize petunias pulling out of the driveway, or gotten distracted and missed your subway stop.

From "drop off dry cleaning" to "remind the boss about his anniversary," your task list may get long—but the organization may actually help you save time in the long run. After all, how many times have you had to run back to the store to pick up dog food after you just stopped for some milk and bread? And it's always faster to list everything at once so you can create a mental map that saves not only time, but gas money. No more running across town to pick up your watch on Monday only to realize you could have dropped off those files to your accountant on the same trip.

Having a blank tape may also allow you to talk out loud, free-forming thoughts and ideas that might not otherwise make it to paper. If you never have time to write in your journal, try keeping an audio journal instead. Not too loud, though—especially if you use public transportation to get to and from work.

Remember that great idea you had on the way to work last month that was lost forever when you heard your favorite song from high school playing on the morning show? And what about the perfect title for your autobiography that just flew out the window along with that piece of paper you were scribbling on at sixty miles per hour? You get the idea.

Be sure to announce the day and date on the tape before you launch into your to-do list. That way when you play it back and hear yourself command, "FedEx proposal by five o'clock today!" you'll know exactly when stuff on your list was supposed to get done.

Likewise, you'll want to have dates in case you need to prove that your brilliant solution to the energy crisis was in fact your idea first.

And unlike paper lists, there's less of a chance of losing your ideas, breakthroughs, and "have-to-do-today-or-lose-my-job" necessities when you record them on tape. Just be sure you either carry your recorder in your purse or leave it in your car or you'll have to add "buy new tape recorder" to tomorrow's to-do list.

Finally, you should listen to that taped to-do list you had the foresight to make. Try right after you arrive at work, or do it on your lunch break.

17

At First Glance

Be prepared to make a good first impression.

"Being on the tightrope is living; everything else is waiting."
—Karl Wallenda

Choking on a crouton. An unexpected belch. A huge zit in the middle of your forehead. These are all things that can make a bad first impression—and unfortunately, they're usually out of your control.

Now that we've covered the "uncontrollables," let's focus on what you *can* do (or *not* do!) to make a good first impression.

First, hygiene. At a job, meeting, or lunch with a client, you need to look your best. This means dressing well, having tidy hair and makeup, and looking put-together.

* Always iron your clothes, even if you think something, like the back of your shirt, won't be seen. The one time you oversleep and skip ironing the back of your blouse will be the time that the office AC is broken. With temps over one hundred degrees, any client will think it bizarre that you refuse to remove your suit jacket. There is now a quick, no-iron spray that allows you to spritz your blouse and tug out the major wrinkles. If you're frequently running late, you may want to invest in a bottle.

* Always keep a stain remover in your purse, briefcase, or glove compartment for unexpected spills. They come in applicator bottles, spray bottles, and even individually wrapped wipes.
* Ditto for clear nail polish, which works great at stopping a run in your nylons from progressing (or keep a spare set of panty hose).
* Hair spray works great in a pinch for static. Keep a tiny bottle in your purse for those times your skirt or slacks latch on to your hose (much like that clingy boyfriend from ninth grade).
* If you tend to wear high heels, keep a set of black flats in your car in case a heel breaks or you get stuck walking a long distance.
* A travel size deodorant is always a necessity; no telling what you'll smell like when you realize (as you pull into your client's parking lot) that you've grabbed the wrong file and will have to wing it!

Now that you look (and smell) great, you can focus on your initial greeting.

A firm handshake is a must, as is eye contact—before, during, and after your meeting.

Timeliness is always important. Getting to a lunch meeting early will allow you not only to check your teeth, hair, makeup, and clothes, but also to make sure that the table is comfortable and appropriate.

If your client is heavyset, for example, you may want to arrive early to ask for a table rather than a booth. Whenever possible, however, this should be done in advance.

Likewise, if you will be discussing confidential company information, you may want to request a booth rather than a centrally located table.

You'll also want to be careful about what you order. Finger foods—such as chicken wings—can make your fingers too greasy to touch paperwork. Sandwiches may be less greasy, but could leave you dripping food on your outfit. Your best bet is something that can be eaten with a fork.

Ordering alcohol may come across as tacky. By letting your client order first, you'll allow him or her to set the boundaries. If your guest orders a glass of wine, don't feel obligated to order alcohol. If you do choose to have alcohol, limit yourself to one glass. Alcohol loosens lips, impairs judgment, impedes your ability to drive, and could get you in trouble later if for some reason you lose the account.

Making a good first impression will largely fall on how prepared and in-control you appear. Having copies for the client, handouts at the meeting, and charts, graphs, and statistics to back up your ideas will certainly make it look as if you've done your homework. Men often process new information visually, rather than aurally. They like tangible, graphic images and handouts, and want to hear about the "bottom line," i.e., "How much will it cost or save me?"

If you're presenting or meeting with a man or group of men, "playing their game" doesn't have to mean compromising anything. On the contrary, it just means helping them to better understand just how brilliant your ideas are.

18

Feliz Navidad!

Plan the ultimate holiday office party.

> *"Never give a party if you will be
> the most interesting person there."*
> **—Mickey Friedman**

A festive and cheery bash is just the ticket for boosting morale, getting to know your coworkers, and scoring brownie points with
your boss. Throw a few platefuls of munchies and a gaggle of coworkers into a room, pipe in some holiday tunes, and you have yourself an
office party!

After getting the thumbs-up from the big cheese, proceed at first
with a bit of caution. To keep from offending Wiccan Wanda, Jewish
Josephine, and Islamic Isabel, tell coworkers you're planning a year-
end holiday party rather than a Christmas bash. Announcing your
intentions in the most politically correct way possible guarantees
nobody will feel left out or otherwise offended. Hey, if they don't feel
like playing along, that just means more avocado dip for you!

Do you have a few coworker chums who are also brimming with
holiday cheer? Enlist them by putting a sign-up sheet on the cafeteria
door! If you choose to go the potluck route, ask everybody to bring a
dish. Better yet, hit up your boss for a party allowance when she's in
a good mood. Most offices have a little petty cash to throw around, so
convince your manager to throw some bucks toward a party platter,

pop, and door prizes. If she's a tough sell, stress that it'll be good PR for management.

Once the food and drink bases are covered, remember to sign up to reserve a conference room or office in which to throw this swank bash. Wouldn't it suck to go to all this trouble, then have to park your cheese platter in the hallway next to the bathroom for lack of space?

You've covered most of the office party dos. Now here's an office party don't: don't serve alcohol! It is tempting to pop a bottle of bubbly in celebration of the season—and to toast the Friday afternoon you spent partying instead of tackling work—but it just takes one goofball barfing in the lobby potted plant or making cracks to the busty secretary to poop on your party. Focus on copping a good sugar buzz off your cubicle mate's almond bars instead!

19

The Butcher, the Baker, the Candlestick-Maker

Make thoughtful yet inexpensive gifts for your coworkers.

"Sainthood is acceptable only in saints."
—**Pamela Hansford Johnson**

Whether your office has ten or one hundred employees, gifts for coworkers can really add up. Even if you draw names for holiday gift-giving, there are bound to be one or two additional people you'll still want to give gifts to. Besides, everyone has a birthday!

Take Sharon, the vice president's receptionist, who has four kids. You know she could really benefit from a mixed bundle of handmade aromatherapy soaps to treat herself to some time alone. And Chuck in the warehouse would be touched to know that you remembered not only his birthday, but the fact that he volunteers at the Humane Society on Saturdays and would love to take the dogs some of your home-made bones.

You've made it your business (without being nosy!) to get to know your coworkers, and creating just the right gift for just the right person is something that you can enjoy year-round.

So what exactly are good, safe gifts to make that won't get you in trouble with the harassment board or have the staff questioning your intentions? ("What are you trying to do, poison us so you can move up in the company?") First, the nonfood items: soaps, candles, and handmade earrings are good general gifts for birthdays and holidays—especially for women. Pillows work for men if they're obsessed with a sports team or activity such as fishing. Ditto with T-shirts that can be screen-printed or lettered with funny sayings or nicknames.

New parents can appreciate something that acknowledges their new arrival—baby clothes for the mom or a cigar or chocolate cigar for the dad. (Or vice versa—depending on the family.)

Frames are always a good gift—as long as the person has kids, dogs, or an object he or she is in love with (boat/car/motorcycle). You can usually purchase a small, generic, desk-appropriate frame for less than five dollars and then decorate it with beads, shells, paint, or stickers.

Ditto with coffee mugs. If you can't find one that has just the right saying or cartoon, make your own! Ceramic paint is cheap—just make sure it's safe for the microwave.

Of course, you can't go wrong with food gifts (well, almost never). You don't want to give your famous milk chocolate truffles to a diabetic coworker; likewise with your ten-hour toffee and the nut-allergic half of the staff.

What you can do, however, is ask ahead of time for a list of allergies or dietary restrictions. This can easily be done under the guise of an upcoming staff luncheon. You could also ask the human resources person to tell you if, say, Jamie is allergic to nuts. Explain your predicament and you're bound to get some help. After all, everyone loves gifts, and the HR manager isn't afraid to tell you she's a chocoholic.

Ready to Get Started?

- Consider finding a favorite family recipe (or download one from the Web) for muffins or mini bread loaves. Attach the recipe—on a pretty card—to the nicely wrapped goodie.

- Everyone loves cookies! Make oversize cookies with a special message written for the person: "Happy Birthday to Our Favorite Chocoholic" might be too long, but "Chocolate Rules!" might work.
- If you have a green thumb, consider cutting starter pieces from house-plants and giving them in cute hand-painted, inexpensive vases or pots.
- Instead of giving an empty frame, cut out a photo of someone (or something) famous depending on the recipient's taste and interests.

20

Community Fun(d)

Get the office to volunteer together and reach out to others.

> "In spite of everything, I still believe that
> people are really good at heart."
> —Anne Frank

Feeling sort of down in the dumps lately? Can't find the perfect pair of Italian leather pumps to go with the suit you picked out for the party? Believe it or not, some poor souls don't have any shoes . . . heck, some people don't even have two functioning feet! (See how lucky you feel already?)

You and your office mates can do a wealth of good for those less fortunate, as well as offer something valuable to the community. You don't have to sacrifice all your worldly possessions (or those Italian pumps, for that matter) to foster a personal sense of pride and score some great press for your company, too.

Here are a few simple ideas for getting the office to pitch in on a volunteer project together. Each of these suggestions gives folks a chance to help firsthand, so everybody gets to bask in the feel-good vibe of giving. Don't forget to invite your local TV and radio stations; they're always looking for human interest stories.

* Everybody loves animals! Is there a Humane Society or Dumb Friends League in your town? Gather a group to go walk the

dogs at the local kennel, or pitch in to buy the shelter some much-needed dog and cat food and leashes.

* Jimmy Carter's Habitat for Humanity has for years been helping to build houses for those less fortunate. These large-scale house-building projects are perfect for those seeking to do good in a single afternoon with a group of colleagues. Check H for H's website (habitat.org) for projects in your area, and don't forget to snap a photo of your company's group with hammers in hand for the company newsletter!

* Contact a few of the different bakeries or delis in town to donate their day-old bread. Assign each coworker a bakery, and meet to drop the bread off at the local homeless shelter. Or, buy food tokens at the mission and distribute them to homeless people downtown.

* Even folks who have very little spare time or money to give can do good. Leave a box for collecting canned goods, and once a month, take turns dropping the box off at the local food bank.

* Often, people who need a little help don't have the resources to dress properly for that all-important job interview. Ask fellow employees to bring in their old suits or business clothes on a designated day, and donate the clothing to a nonprofit that offers vocational rehabilitation.

* Want a more hands-on help experience? Get everyone to bake cookies or make sandwiches, then take your lunch hour to stroll through downtown and hand them out to the homeless.

* Women's shelters always need basic supplies for those in need. Get everyone to pitch in a set amount (say five or ten dollars each), go buy a bunch of towels and toiletries, and deliver them to a women's shelter.

Before you embark on such a project, be sure to get input from your coworkers; getting their thumbs-up will ensure you're not the only one who shows up in your grubbies on Volunteer Saturday.

Where to Begin?

Check out Volunteers of America at voa.org, or try networkforgood.org for more ideas.

21

Secrets of a Discount Queen

Take initiative to negotiate vendor discounts
for your company.

> *"Everybody gets so much information all day long
> that they lose their common sense."*
> **—Gertrude Stein**

Who better to negotiate deals than the most diplomatic, gentle yet firm employee at your company—you?!

No, we're not talking about getting your suppliers in Japan to sell you their new line for $6 million instead of $9 million. We're talking about your ability to sniff out a bargain, use the power of group buying, and talk your way into a well-deserved 10 percent off for prompt payment to long-standing accounts.

You don't have to be a salesperson, accountant, or big-deal negotiator to save your company and its employees hundreds (even thousands) of dollars. You just need to ask.

Take your gym, for example. You've run into a few employees amidst your Wednesday night workout, and a few more have indicated that they might be interested in joining (with much credit due to your fit, svelte self!). Why not talk to your gym's manager and ask if he'd cut you a group rate if you get, say ten or more employees to join? Even though you're already a member, getting your coworkers signed up could cut your monthly fee or perhaps omit your yearly membership cost. If nothing else, it may give you some new workout partners!

If your firm hires the same catering company for all its events, why not ask the owner for a regular-client discount of say, 5 percent? If you're careful not to appear as though you're threatening them, vendors may see the offer as a great way to increase their business knowing your company will almost always use them in the future.

The same goes for hotels and rental car businesses. If your company frequently has out-of-town clients visiting, ask the hotel for regular-customer discounts or free upgrades. A suite instead of a room, a midsize car instead of a compact car, or a free breakfast with a room rental can help your company pamper a client with no extra cost.

If you frequently hold awards banquets, business expos, or training seminars outside the office, talk to the venue coordinator about the possibility of an exclusive-user discount. Ask for an hourly discount if your company rents the space more than four times per year.

The same goes for rental companies for your firm's frequent use of projectors, big screen monitors, microphones, or banquet tables.

Even day-care providers may be open to the possibility of group discounts. If your company has thirty working parents and no on-site child-care provider, contact a few places near the office and ask if they'd be willing to offer a company discount for the employees.

Planning to attend a large convention, concert, or business expo? Many large functions offer discounts for purchases of ten or more tickets. Call in advance to confirm how many tickets you need to buy, then start a sign-up sheet at work.

You may need to collect the money in advance, though. You don't want to get stuck with a $400 charge on your credit card only to have everyone back out at the last minute. Trusting your coworkers is a nice gesture, but taking precautions is a smart move.

Did you know...

Metal paper clips alone account for an annual U.S. steel consumption of ten thousand tons. Lloyd's Bank of London undertook an extraordinary study to discover exactly what happens to a typical batch of paper clips in their office building. Out of the original batch of 100,000 clips, 3,196 were used as pipe cleaners; 5,308 were used as nail cleaners; 5,434 were used to pick teeth or scratch ears; 19,413 served as card game chips; 14,163 were snapped, broken, or otherwise twisted useless during phone conversations; 7,200 were used as hooks for belts, suspenders, or bras; and 25,000 became casualties lost in odd office crevices, swept up, or otherwise disappeared. All in all, only 20,000 out of the original 100,000 were used to clip paper.

22

Charity of the Month

Pick one charity a month for you and
your coworkers to contribute to.

"He is rich who hath enough to be charitable."
—Sir Thomas Browne

If a journey of a thousand miles begins with just one step, raising a thousand bucks or more for a good cause begins with just one buck. For just a fraction of the cost of latte and biscotti that goes straight to your thighs anyway, you could be housing Haitian orphans, feeding Romanian refugees, or performing some other lofty service.

Most of us want to help out, we really do. Between working, playing, and leading our busy lives, however, helping those less fortunate gets put off as something to do "someday." Maybe someday is today! And just think: if you got a few coworkers to pitch in too, you could be multiplying that do-good money in no time. By taking the reins and proactively asking others to help out, you might be on the fast track to Mother Theresa–hood in no time.

The best way to approach your coworkers is informally, with a soft sell. Some straitlaced companies have gobs of rules about soliciting coworkers or raising money for causes that don't jive with their corporate culture. If your place of employment's strict rules, regulations, and long list of no-no's make starting a charity pool feel more grueling than an IRS audit, do it surreptitiously between buddy workers rather than hitting up a whole department. Do a few of you bust out for lunch off-site occasionally? Know a few cool people from the softball league? Chances are if you're feeling generous and wanting to contribute to the good of humanity, they might be too.

No need to start a grandiose project, either (though those orphans would appreciate it). Here are a few suggestions that may get everyone started with a minimum of angst:

* Do you have a regular lunch group that goes out twice a week? Switch from pop to water once a week, and throw the buck everyone saves into the kitty.
* Do you have a change jar going at home? So do the people you work with. Volunteer to take everyone's change to your local bank and have them count it in their coin counting machine. Ask the teller to give you a money order for the proceeds, and send it off. Better yet, put a change jar in the office kitchen so people don't even have to bring it from home. No "borrowing" for pops, either.
* Do you get reimbursed for mileage and miscellaneous expenses? Those measly checks are nice to get, but not a necessity like your paycheck. Rather than throwing a piddly check for $4.67 in your account, throw even one such check into the till each month and ask your work buddies to do the same.

Keep everyone informed of how much you gathered during the month and what charity it was sent to, so all can bask in that warm, fuzzy feeling. To spread the wealth, pick a different charity each time. Let a different contributor choose the charity each month to avoid head-butting about whose cause is more worthy. Rotating charities means they all get a piece of the pie.

When you get home and your honey says, "What did you do today?" you'll be able to brag, "I filed, finished my quarterly report, and helped save the world."

Cool Websites

Want to contribute to a charity but don't know where to start? Check out charitywatch.com or networkforgood.org to find organizations that help specific causes.

23

Heating Up Cold Calls

Become a growing asset by finding sales leads
for your company.

"I've been rich and I've been poor; rich is better."
—Sophie Tucker

No matter what your position in the company, finding leads is always helpful, as long as you don't step on any toes. Hot prospects can not only help your company obtain new clients (and therefore make more money), but can also help your chances of receiving a promotion, pay raise, or larger commission.

Your first step is to find out just what is a good lead for your company; new businesses, growing companies, organizations with a larger IT staff, or perhaps companies with a staff of more than one hundred.

There are several ways to learn just what your sales team is looking for. The first one is to ask the sales manager. Assuming the manager doesn't feel threatened, he or she may be happy to share information with you. After all, money in a salesperson's pocket is always an incentive, but so is meeting or exceeding his or her sales quota.

Be clear—and honest—about your intentions. If you're hoping for a commission, say so. Some salespeople are happy to pay out a referral fee when a prospect leads to a sale. After all, 90 percent of a sales commission (assuming he or she paid out 10 percent) is better than 100 percent of zero!

If you run into a roadblock—i.e., a salesperson who sees your question as a threat—feel free to ask your boss. Explain your intention and that your search for leads will merely help the company without taking you away from your duties. Give specific examples on how you can search for prospects without neglecting your current responsibilities. Some ideas might include:

* "I had a few minutes after I finished research for the Hope account on the Internet. I ran across five companies in town that are expanding. Would you like more information, such as contact names and phone numbers?"

* "I was reading an article in *BusinessWeek* about some of the latest companies to go public with their stock. Does that indicate that they're growing? If so, would you like details?"

* "I just discovered a new local business publication that lists companies that have opened in the last ninety days. Would this be of interest to you?"

* "One of the trade magazines had a review of the Top 25 Movers and Shakers in our industry. Would you like a copy?"

* "I checked out our competition's website and learned that they're tapping into new markets. The ideas seem like something our company might want to consider. Would you like me to summarize their plans for you?"

* "I just read a great book on how many companies have neglected the growing number of women over fifty. Would you like me to gather some statistics for our next sales meeting?"

Your boss would be crazy to not at least hear (or read) your ideas. Just be sure to document your research and make copies for at least one other person in the office in case your boss neglects to mention to *his* boss that you're the brains behind "his" latest idea.

You'll also want to keep a copy for yourself. When it's time for your evaluation, you'll have plenty of documentation that you're a continuing asset to a growing company.

24

Brown Bag Brainiacs

Start an in-office financial club that meets
one lunch hour a month.

*"I do everything for a reason.
Most of the time the reason is money."*
—Suzy Parker

Interest rates. Mutual funds. Employee stock options. Financial lingo can seem pretty intimidating to those of us with plain old checking and savings accounts.

We want to learn about money, we really do. We picture ourselves with sophisticated stuff like stocks, investment portfolios, and other foreign-sounding financial boons. It's usually when we get a bounced check statement in the mail or run across a feel-good article in the paper, "Single Mom Puts 7 Kids Through School by Scrubbing Floors," that we think, "Hey, I need to become more money savvy." Many of us didn't take finance in college, so the burden of becoming money goddesses falls to each of us.

If finances befuddle you, chances are the rest of your coworkers feel the same way. Why not gather your colleagues and join an investment club so you can get savvy about saving as a group?

First, a few basic guidelines are in order. An investment club isn't like a book club, where everybody congregates once a month to yap about the book at hand (although a book club that focuses on reading and discussing finance books sounds like a really good idea). Investment clubs are groups where each member pays to participate, and the group takes the pot of money to invest in various stocks. The piddly amount you'll be asked to pay pales in comparison to the wealth of practical experience you get through the club. Usually, all members participate in picking and researching new stocks, monitoring the performance of existing stocks, and plotting a course of action on dud investments.

Clubs differ, but the goal is usually the same—to learn the subtleties of the stock market, mutual funds, annuities, and other investments while collectively earning a little on the side, too. Most investment clubs, whether they're an officially recognized organization or not, take any earnings the club makes and reinvest them. Which brings up an interesting point: what happens to your money once you decide to leave the club? Besides getting your initial investment back, how does the club organizer determine what dividends, if any, you receive as well? And last but not least, who's handling and keeping the funds? You want to hear that there are safeguards in place to make sure your money is handled wisely, without unknowingly taking a chance that the investment club manager is actually some fly-by-night ex-convict who's wanted in eighteen states for embezzlement.

These types of clubs are easy to find, once you know where to look. Try your alumni association or college, since many clubs exist at the student level. Ask around at your next professional association meeting if you belong to any trade groups. If you belong to a bank or have access to a financial advisor, see if they can point you in the right direction.

What will you get in return for your investment clubbing? Stock market smarts that will pay dividends for decades down the road, allowing you to serve as your own financial adviser. Not too shabby!

It's About the Money, Honey

Check out these websites today and start building your money finesse:

- smartmoney.com
- youngmoney.com
- money.com

25

At Your Service

Deal with rude customers effectively.

> *"Never eat more than you can lift."*
> **—Miss Piggy**

"This steak is overcooked!"

"Lemme talk to the owner."

"So I broke it. Give me a new one."

Sound familiar? Working with the public can be a daunting task—especially if you have to do it every day. Whether you're a waitress, retail clerk, receptionist, or CEO, dealing with less-than-polite people can leave you with a headache and a desire to join a convent.

Still, there are ways to turn a bad situation good—even with the toughest of the complainers.

For most companies, the rule is "The customer is always right." This ordinance actually gives you a lot of power, as your company will most likely back you up if you do whatever it takes to satisfy the client.

With this in mind, your first step should be to give the customer your full attention. Listen to the customer's complaint in order to understand not only what's wrong, but what the customer wants done to remedy the situation. If the solution is within your means, say so.

"So, the radio you purchased isn't working? Sounds like we need to give you a replacement at no charge. Thanks for bringing this to our attention. We'll have someone notify the manufacturer."

Sometimes the problem is more difficult to correct, as the customer doesn't have a solution in mind. This situation is a bit trickier, because you'll have to come up with possible solutions.

"Well, since you don't want another steak and you weren't satisfied with this one, how about if we just take it off your bill?"

If your first solution doesn't appear to calm down the customer, you may have to add a second solution.

"Perhaps in addition to taking the steak off your bill, we could give you a free dessert to take home."

If this still doesn't work, don't assume it's because the customer just isn't being cooperative. The person could, after all, be heading to a movie or on a diet—in which case a free dessert sitting in his or her car for two hours might not be appealing.

Offering a gift certificate to ensure that customers return is a great idea if they're not tourists from out of state. If they're locals (or tourists with relatives who are locals), be sure to insist that they specifically ask for you or a manager when they return so that you can make sure they're taken care of. As studies show that customers who have a bad experience will tell ten people, you're not risking losing just one or two customers, but nine (and everyone else they would have brought).

Oftentimes, the customer just wants his or her complaint heard. If this is the case, listen without defending yourself, another employee, the product, or the company. If the customer still seems upset after "venting," you may want to offer to get a manager. Sometimes just talking to someone the customer perceives as "the boss" makes him or her feel better. It could be because the customer suspects that a worker wouldn't report the incident to a higher-up for fear of getting reprimanded or fired. Don't take it personally. A lot of what customers react to is from past experiences. Just do your best to make sure this isn't one they remember for the wrong reasons.

26

Stop Procrastinating!

Develop a strategy for doing it now.

"No idleness, no laziness, no procrastination: never put off till tomorrow what you can do today."
—Earl of Chesterfield

You have dreams and goals . . . you're going places, girl! Between your personal plans, your career, and your hopes for the future, you have a lot planned.

But not today. No, today you're tired/crabby/drained/PMSing/depressed and can only operate on a 50 percent energy level. After all, you can't *really* be expected to set the world aflame with your ragged cuticles, stack of bills, and sagging energy, can you? Better to just wait until tomorrow. Tomorrow, you'll feel peppier. Tomorrow will be a whole different story. Or maybe the day after . . .

And so it goes with procrastination. All those well-intentioned long- and short-term goals don't do a whole lot of good if they don't get acted upon. Intentions are great, but action is what makes dreams a reality.

Procrastination can be anything from leaving important tasks until the last minute, to dillydallying days away, keeping you distracted from your hoped-for achievements. Experts disagree whether procrastination is an innate behavior or simply a nagging habit, but there's a very good reason for stopping procrastination: it keeps you from enjoying the happiness gleaned from achieving your goals.

Take your future into your own hands, and choose a few of these time-tested antiprocrastination techniques—and think of at least two other tricks that might work for you . . . right now!

1. **Set a schedule.** Don't wait for inspiration to strike and sit around waiting for your muse to arrive. Work on your tasks at the same time each day. Soon your body will say, "It's seven o'clock, must be time to write/paint/work on my proposal." Before you know it, tackling tasks will seem automatic.

2. **Do yucky tasks first.** Taking a deep breath and plunging through your least favorite chores (making tough phone calls, handling complaints) gets them off your plate and does away with that gnawing sense of dread that accompanies having such tasks hang around till the end of your "things to do today."

3. **Break the task into achievable chunks.** Writing the great American novel or scoring your M.B.A. is *huge*, right? Not really, when you break it down: write just three pages a day and you'll have a three-hundred-page manuscript in less than four months. Four classes a semester means you'll be putting "M.B.A." on your résumé in around two years.

4. **Lock yourself into your office and eliminate distractions.** No coffee, bathroom breaks, or office banter for you until you finish. Then turn off the phone, shut the office door, and stop playing with the radio. Produce results instead of trying to find that funky AM jazz station or checking your personal E-mail box. No exceptions!

5. **Reward yourself for completion.** "When I get this screenplay done, I'm buying those cool boots I saw at the mall."

6. **Visualize the end result.** Will completing this task get you closer to the job/project/lifestyle of your dreams? That should be reason enough to get started!

7. **Be accountable.** Find a similarly motivated buddy, and keep each other accountable for tasks. It's harder to slack when you have someone breathing down your neck.

8. **Ritualize it.** Find sensory delights that correspond with your work, and use them only to get you into that zone. For example, if switching on the lava lamp says, "OK, time to make some calls!" or a cup of chai tea says, "Yummy . . . must be time to tackle that research," use those internal signals to help get you there.

Remember, strive for production, not perfection. Before investing too heavily in a certain task, ask, "How much of my time is this worth? What's the worst that could happen if I shave a few minutes off?" Keeping these questions at the forefront of your brain keeps you focused on finishing, rather than following a tangent into perfectionistic behavior that wastes time, such as rewriting and editing memos that are insignificant, or recording and erasing the same voice mail six times because you don't like the sound of your voice.

Now go tackle that project you've been putting off!

27

Wisdom in the Workplace

Start a wisdom circle with open-minded office mates who seek input for life's little challenges.

> *"Wisdom doesn't automatically come with old age. Nothing does—except wrinkles. It's true, some wines improve with age. But only if the grapes were good in the first place."*
> **—Abigail Van Buren**

Should you really apply for that other job? Does E-marketing really work? Bill Gates or Donald Trump—who had better business plans? These are the pressing questions of the universe. If only you had additional brains to help you sort out life's Big Questions . . . but can you really trust your girlfriends with such weighty matters when their deepest philosophical question is whether horizontal stripes truly add ten pounds or not?

Chances are your coworkers may be pondering such questions, too. Start a wisdom circle with other confidentiality-respecting cubicle mates and you'll have built a circle of smarties to help you sort out life's biggest issues!

Wisdom circles have been around forever (just ask Native Americans). It wasn't until the modern age arrived that we decided we could all figure this stuff out on our own, thank you very much. Think of how we'd be able to tackle tough issues and get valuable input to boot if we pondered stuff as a group rather than alone. Why not take advantage of the fact that you're snared in a building with the same people five days a week?

A wisdom circle can be structured or very loose, depending on the personalities of the group. Each person brings a question, any question, to the group for input and advice. Different from a discussion group where everyone yaps at length, think of a wisdom circle as a gaggle of objective pals who pitch in their two cents about a question or problem. The only structure should be a two- or three-minute time limit (yes, bring a kitchen timer!) on both the question and each person's response, so everyone gets to share her or his pearls of wisdom equally.

Say one person needs help handling a difficult client (or wants to save the company more money, or learn to think positively) and seeks techniques from the group. Go around the room and give everyone a few minutes to suggest solutions, with the understanding that the purpose is to give constructive advice, not to condemn or chime in about unrelated stuff. Then the next person poses her or his one question and the process starts all over.

Start by inviting a few friendly coworkers to do lunch with the idea of starting a wisdom circle. While it's easy to start with just a few folks, six people works well (too many, and you'll be there all day).

One caveat when "wisdoming" with colleagues: be careful what you blab to the group. Save the superpersonal stuff for your shrink, and don't share private details about other coworkers. Getting tips on how to stop procrastinating is one thing, but blurting out "I can't believe George and Helen in the HR department are having an affair!" is sure to make everyone very uncomfortable. Stick to business-related topics and don't cross any lines that might be construed as "spilling the company's beans."

Instead, opt for ideas that need more brainstorming than yes-or-no responses. Things like "How can we grow our target market?" or "What can we do to increase traffic to the company's website?" are good questions to get great minds thinking alike—and differently.

28

Read Your Way to the Top

Subscribe to industry mags to get the inside scoop.

> *"Read, every day, something no one else is reading. Think, every day, something no one else is thinking. Do, every day, something no one else would be silly enough to do. It is bad for the mind to continually be part of unanimity."*
> **—Christopher Morley**

You're sitting in a staff meeting, racking your brain for something intelligent to contribute to the conversation. It's your big chance to make an impression on the regional supervisor and score points within your department, but all you can think of to say is, "When are they gonna restock the M&Ms in the third-floor vending machine? It's been out for over a week."

Don't let this happen to you. Pick up an industry rag or two to read between big projects, or to kill time on the bus. Before you know it, you'll be spouting pithy insights and obscure industry-related data that'll soon earn you a reputation as a business insider.

"Industry mags?" you ask. "Where would I find such publications? Anyway, I'm a bicycle messenger/temp/short-order cook. They probably don't make magazines for workers like me."

You would be surprised! Industry magazines, also called trade magazines, are for anyone eager to learn more about the ups, downs, and future of a certain industry. While these magazines aren't aimed at the general public (after all, how many regular folks really care about the new state trucking regulations featured in *Overdrive* magazine?), they provide all sorts of marketing, employment, and new product details specific to your niche that'll keep you in the know. Better yet, trade publications give you an inside view of an industry you might be thinking of breaking into.

Don't look for these publications on the rack next to *Time*, though. Most of these publications are available by subscription only—and some of them are so choosy about who's peeking into their field that they place restrictions on who can subscribe! The best place to start is with your professional association, if you have one. Many professional organizations publish their own magazine or newsletter, offering it as one of the perks of joining.

No association membership? No problem. Try Googling to get the names of a few of the trade rags you might be interested in (try a general search with your job title and the word *magazine* such as "hairdresser magazine" to see what pops up). Just because your publication doesn't appear on an Internet search doesn't mean it doesn't exist, however. Next time you're at the library, look for a rather dry reference tome titled *Business Publication Advertising Source*, which features a compendium of details on various trade publications.

Wondering just what kind of trade magazines exist? Check out these titles:

* For airline industry workers: *Aviation International News* at ain-online.com covers many aspects of the commercial airline industry.
* Want to work in a spa? First, check out *Day Spa* magazine at dayspamagazine.com for an inside look at salons.
* *Foreword* magazine (forewordmagazine.com) tells librarians, bookstore workers, and other publication peddlers all they could ever want to know about independent presses.

* *Conference Board* magazine at conference-board.org can help coach any aspiring Corporate Sally to that higher echelon of power.
* Thinking of starting your own venture? Check out *Minority Business Entrepreneur* at mbemag.com for the inside scoop on how to ensure your success.
* Do you spend nine to five in a cubicle? Check out *Office Solutions*, the magazine for office professionals (os-od.com) for a peek into the mind of the typical office manager.
* There's even a magazine for Port a Potty operators! The *Portable Restroom Operator* can be found at 1promag.com. There's something to put on the back of your toilet at home.

29

Corporate Kiddies

Rally for on-site day care for working mommies.

"The best way to predict the future is to invent it."
—Alan Kay

Think Meryl Streep in *Silkwood* or Julia Roberts in *Erin Brockovich*. No, we're not talking about push-up bras, we're trying to conjure images of strong, brave women, fighting for the rights of innocent people and doing the right thing even under pressure from Corporate Conglomerate ABC.

You don't have to be a famous movie star to walk in the footsteps of these empowered women. (After all, both movies were based on true stories.) What you *do* have to be is tough, focused, and ticked off enough to want to change things around your office.

This is not to say that you should go looking for a fight. On the contrary. Only pursue the battles you feel are in need of a lobbyist. On a more selfish note, you could also choose the wars that will improve your own life significantly.

Take the mommy issue, for example.

Being a woman yourself, you've noticed a true lack of attention to the day-care issue. There are plenty of moms at your office struggling to keep up with the high cost of day care. You've watched Dinah, a single mother of three, suffer long enough—trying to survive off what little amount of money she has left from her paycheck after day-care costs. She brings a bag lunch, drives an old car, and shops in thrift shops. Well, sisters unite! What you need is an on-site day-care facility, and you're just the woman to get the idea off the ground!

Approaching your boss will take some skill and diligence. You may want to have a preexisting location picked out to make the project less costly. Surely there's a space in your building that just screams day care (or better yet, has padded walls to muffle the screams of crying children!). What about the giant storage room that's merely holding papers from the company's first five years in business during the Carter administration? Couldn't those archives be kept in a storage facility for a mere $100 a month? And couldn't your company use another good benefit for those prospective new employees?

You could rally the moms for a brainstorming party to get input, ideas, and even discounts for designing the day-care center. "Joyce, doesn't your husband own a contracting company? And Betty, your sister owns a carpet store, right?" You may be amazed to learn how quickly your idea can be made a reality.

Of course, you may have to be willing to put in more than your two cents. In theory, the idea is great, but you may have to go it alone. No sense fighting your boss to cough up the cash only to expect someone else to step up to the planning plate. After all, just because your coworkers may want the day-care center doesn't mean they have time to draw up blueprints. They do have *kids*, remember?

30

Memo-bilia

Spice up company memos and newsletters with humor.

> *"Satire should like a polished razor keen,*
> *Wound with a touch that's scarcely felt or seen."*
> —**Mary Wortley Montagu**

From bright purple iMacs to zippy gel pens, plain old office supplies are becoming more fun. It's a sure sign the office deities are starting to smile upon us lowly office workers.

Too bad that spirited sense of fun doesn't extend to the typical office memo or newsletter. The majority of offices are still distributing the written word as plain old memorandums on dull white or beige paper . . . yawn! No wonder nobody reads that stuff! Savvy workers and managers realize it's not a crime to use a little panache when it comes to office communication. Professional doesn't have to mean devoid of personality, punch, and pizzazz.

It's time to laugh at work, and not just when you get your paycheck! Spice up the company newsletter or memo with a little humor, and your coworkers will surely be thanking you for the needed smile. Plus managers will be thanking you for the extra effort that was fun for you anyway. If you're a secretary or PR chick who dreads putting out the internal newsletter month after month, take heart! Don't think of the company-wide newsletter as a mandatory waste of trees, but a blank palette awaiting your touch, to be xeroxed for all the world (or at least your immediate sales division) to see!

Are you a humorless lump devoid of a single clever, witty atom in your brain? No problem! Add some clever work-related quotes to prove a point or convey a feeling. Cute-quote dictionaries are a dime a dozen, as are work-related desk calendars with pithy sayings that simply cry out to be spotlighted in your next piece. Dozens of online quotation websites exist for your surfing pleasure. Motivational, inspirational, and humorous quotes all work well here. Better yet, spotlight a quote from one of your fellow workers. Your coworker will be flattered that her or his words were immortalized and important enough to repeat.

Feel OK including some humor? Try reporting the necessary facts with a lighthearted and readable touch. You may have to report a bunch of dry sales figures, but nobody says you can't editorialize along the way: "Our sales are down 24 percent this quarter—yikes! But sales manager Jones single-handedly closed eight of our office's ten deals this week. Way to bust a move, Jones!"

Or start your own little side column or regular feature with hot tips from around the neighborhood that surrounds your office building. Word on the street may be that there's a funky new falafel joint opening on the corner, or the dry cleaner on the fourth floor delivers for free. That stuff's all gold to other employees.

Be fun, but err on the side of conservatism if in doubt. Keep the wisecracks generic and universal, rather than too personal by singling out someone, or using religion in either a positive or a negative way, lest some too-sensitive coworker starts complaining. And spare the cutie-pie clip art or other embellishments. The presentation should still be businesslike, not look like you went hog wild at the stamp-booking store.

Keep churning out fun newsletters, and you may get noticed by some key superiors. The next employee you spotlight in the "Congratulations on your promotion!" section could be yourself!

31

♪nappier ♪nack♪

Request healthier choices from the company that stocks
your office vending machine.

*"I've been on a constant diet for the last two decades.
I've lost a total of 789 pounds. By all accounts, I should be
hanging from a charm bracelet."*
—Erma Bombeck

Have you ever noticed that when you crave chocolate you can't find
any, and when you're trying to eat healthy all you can find is chocolate? It's no coincidence. There's a logical explanation: your office
vending machine is always filled with junk food but the chocolate is
missing when you're PMSing because all the other women in your
office are also PMSing (haven't you read about synchronized cycles?)
and their offices are closer to the break room than yours.

The chocolate drought is an easy problem to fix: buy it and keep it
in your drawer until you *do* get a craving.

The lack of healthy snacks isn't quite so easy.

First, you'll need to find out who the vendor is. If you're not already
in charge of calling the company when you're critically low on the
boss's favorite honey buns, you can probably find a phone number on
the machine someplace. Calling and asking to speak to someone about
your healthier snack options is the easy part. It's getting your coworkers to agree that's going to be tough. Before you even begin the uphill

battle, call the vending company and ask for a list of what *is* available in the way of non–junk food. You may learn that the company only has junk—which could save you the trouble of arguing with coworkers and getting hate mail from Hyper Holly in human resources.

Assuming you can, and do, get a list of alternative snacks from the company, review the items to see if anything is even worth fighting for. Dried apples may be healthier than Snickers bars, but if you won't eat them you'll get *twice* the wrath. "You're the one who wanted these stupid healthy snacks, so eat 'em!"

If there are some appealing items, start dropping hints around your office to feel out the rest of the staff and see if you can win any allies. "Janie, I've been thinking. Wouldn't it be nice to have something other than Twinkies in our vending machine? I mean, with summer coming up, I'd like to be able to wear a bathing suit, but I'm a sucker for anything cream-filled."

Don't get too excited if Janie agrees with you. Just because she thinks she eats too many Hostess pies and wants to fit into a swimsuit doesn't mean she's willing to give them up. Talk and action are two completely different things.

Instead, ask for her Janie Hancock if she agrees. Be prepared with a petition to get more healthy snacks in the machine. You may even want to have a list of items that the vending machine company says are "hot sellers" in order to entice anyone who's on the fence. "Val's Vending says that the Nutrigrain bars are great alternatives to the chocolate cupcakes. He also said he can get orange juice in a can to replace the grape soda that nobody drinks anyway. We could really use the vitamin C during cold season, huh?"

Once you get one or two coworkers on your side, you'll have an easier time convincing the others. Just be sure to bring up your idea at a meeting when Hyper Holly is out of town, or you could end up needing that vitamin C to heal the scratch marks on your face.

32

Getting Suggestive

Start a suggestion box for anonymous worker input.

> "The only thing to do with good advice is pass it on.
> It is never any use to oneself."
> —Oscar Wilde

Have you come up with a more efficient way to handle routine paperwork or a great idea for a team-building staff event? Rooting for ten-hour, four-day workweeks and want to make your voice heard without having the managers think you're a slacker? Want your workplace to consider on-site day care for your toddler? Suggest a suggestion box, so you and the rest of the office underlings can make your voices heard!

The humble and amazingly low-tech suggestion box has been around forever, serving as a boon for both workers and managers alike. The concept: allow workers to air their opinions without making a spectacle of themselves, and let managers hear what ordinary folks have to say without sucking up or fearing retribution. As a matter of fact, workplace experts say that one little suggestion box can be a big morale booster, provided the suggestions are reviewed regularly and actually addressed—all except that anonymous "I wish the management would take a management class" suggestion.

Don't have such a wonderful tool at your workplace? Well, get ready to score some points with the team! Next time you're enduring the mandatory company meeting, suggest your business provide a suggestion box, and volunteer to create one. Anything from an empty file box to a shoe box from home will work just fine. Go the extra step and leave some blank memo paper next to the box so it actually gets used.

Post a few ground rules for submission right on the box to encourage coworkers to participate. A few good guidelines are:

* All suggestions are anonymous. (This encourages honest input from employees.)
* Suggestions are reviewed regularly by management. (Nothing will deflate that newfound morale faster than employees feeling like the box is a black hole where their earnestly submitted pleas are never heard.)

Once the workers have done their part, it's time for the bosses to return the favor. When pitching the concept of the suggestion box, volunteer to remove all entries and type them up for managers to consider at monthly meetings, and don't forget to mention when changes are implemented that they originated at the box. That encourages more people to make productive comments on how to improve things.

Here's a twist that works for some smart companies: a suggestion-of- the-month bonus, to get workers to contribute regularly. Of course, anonymity would become optional, since you would *want* your name on an award-winning suggestion. After managers review the entries, they choose the top entry to implement and mass E-mail the suggestion to employees. The employee who made the winning suggestion gets a free coupon, a paid half-day off, or some other treat. So if casual Fridays finally get implemented thanks to your regular whining to the suggestion box, you'll get a pittance prize, too—everybody wins! (Especially the makers of Dockers pants.)

33

Moonlighting Serenade

Work a night job without jeopardizing your day job.

"I wrote the story myself. It's all about a girl who lost her reputation but never missed it."
—Mae West

For many women, just because your office closes at 5 P.M. doesn't mean your day is over. On the contrary, for many, it means your day (or rather your night) is just beginning.

With children (or a shoe fetish) to support, many women are taking on second (and dare we say *third*) jobs to help make ends meet.

As if child care, pet sitting, and sore feet aren't enough, there's one more variable you should factor into the equation: your boss.

Although it may seem unfair, it's your boss's business to know that you're moonlighting. There are plenty of reasons, the top being scheduling, confidentiality, and reputation.

Scheduling can become an issue if one of your jobs requires flexibility, such as overtime or filling in for no-shows. If your nine-to-five needs you to stay late, how will that affect your waitressing shift that starts at 6 P.M.?

Ditto with weekends when restaurants and retail stores are most busy. What if you need to fly to Phoenix for a weekend conference? If you haven't told your boss in advance that you have a second job, the "no-can-do-because-I-never-told-you . . ." explanation will be coming a little too late.

Telling your boss will not only save you from embarrassment (and possibly termination) but may actually lead to a bit more understanding and flexibility.

In addition, some companies actually have a policy against moonlighting. This is sometimes due to a confidentiality agreement—they don't want you casually mentioning that your company is bidding on a big contract, only to find out that the customer you're waiting on is the CEO for the competition.

Some companies also have concerns about their reputation. How would it look if someone learned that the accountant is washing cars for extra cash? The company may have concerns that it will look like it is not paying you enough—or worse, that it can't *afford* to pay you enough.

The good news is that telling your boss you need a second job may earn you a pay raise. At the very least, your boss may wrap up the end-of-the-day meetings on time so you can head home to see your kids before donning your 7-Eleven uniform.

At the worst, your boss will tell you that you can't waitress. If so, ask what type of job he or she *would* approve of. Whenever possible, you'll want to do this *before* you accept that second job offer.

Give your boss some credit—and some insight—and you won't have to be worried if he or she ends up getting seated in your section. Otherwise your only tip might be "Find another job."

34

The Merit of a Mentor

Find someone who has your dream job and
ask her or him to mentor you to the top.

*"Opportunity is missed by most people because
it is dressed in overalls and looks like work."*
—Thomas A. Edison

D o you have a coworker whose job turns you positively green with
envy? Is there someone in your company whose fast-track career
maneuvering lands cherry assignments (and paychecks!) that make
your job look like the pits in comparison? Don't lament your
coworker's luck—learn from her or him! Next time Miss Hotshot
whizzes by your desk en route to some deal-clinching, high-powered
meeting while you're stuck schlepping through old files, stop her in
her tracks and say, "Hey, I want you to be my mentor!"

Getting a mentor is a great way to learn the ins and outs of a business from someone in the know. Plenty of plum jobs are out there for
the picking, if only you know how to land one. Who better to tell you
how to get your dream job than someone who's been there, done that,
and is happy to show you the way?

Gone are the days when mentoring was strictly between fresh-out-
of-college newbies and seasoned business pros. Lots of corporations
today are starting official mentorship programs that help pair people
up within the company as a means of passing on new skills. Getting

your own personal guru could be as easy as signing up with your company's mentor program.

Are you stuck somewhere that doesn't offer such nifty work-related matchmaking? No problem! Finding your own mentor is as easy as: (1) finding someone who's working in a job or area you'd love to know more about, and (2) asking this person to mentor you. Sure, you may feel a little gawky asking your mentor-to-be if you can bask in her or his glory, but you'll likely be surprised by a positive reaction. Your chosen model is certain to be flattered by your request, and since most people love to talk about themselves, their success, and their vast wealth of wisdom, she or he is 99 percent sure to say yes.

In fact, there's no rule that says you can't land a mentor outside your company, if that's where your dream job lies. Whether you're a budding fashionista or a velvet-voiced songbird in waiting, why not hit up Isaac Mizrahi or Mariah Carey for a few tips on how to climb to the top? If the person says no, you're no worse off than before. If he or she says yes, get ready to be molded by a master in the field.

The best part of hooking up with a mentor (besides the hope that some of his or her magic powers will rub off on you) is learning all the little tips and tricks of the trade you didn't learn in school. From "never be caught dead wearing stirrup pants to a job interview" to "Tuesday afternoons are best for cold calling clients," mentors can serve as a bottomless pit of insight.

Although you probably already knew the unwritten rule about never (ever!) wearing stirrup pants . . .

👓 Women in History

Even women who are pioneers in their field have mentors! Firebrand Amelia Earhart learned to fly by taking lessons with aviatrix Anita "Neta" Snook at Kinner Field in California.

35

Sharing the Knowledge

Learn from your coworkers' expertise.

"People are more fun than anybody."
—Dorothy Parker

What makes you think you're so smart? So you have a bachelor's degree in psychology. Big deal! There are plenty of people at your office who are just as intelligent—you just don't know them well enough. Take Marge in the drafting department. She has a Ph.D. in architectural design. And Kevin, the guy who operates the web press—he actually finished law school and passed the Bar on his first try!

Now that you know that you're not the only one who took calculus for the fun of it, why not pool your on-site resources for some free learning? With an endless supply of "smarties" at your company, you have the potential to start a database of knowledge.

Your first task will be to bring the experts together. Hold a "Call for Experts" and just watch the think tank form. Suggest that once a week, a different smartie host a short seminar followed by a question and answer session on his or her topic.

Want to know what recourse you have against the landlord who won't give you back your rental deposit despite the fact that you left the apartment in better shape than you found it? Attend Kevin's Wednesday lunch-hour session and learn your options.

Interested in learning more about what foods will increase your metabolism and help you lose weight? Check out Cheryl's one-hour nutrition workshop and change your eating habits for the better.

And what about you? What are you an expert on? Dressing for success? Passing the GRE with flying colors? Meditation? Mediation? Contract negotiation? Figure out what you do best and offer a short session to help spread your knowledge with the rest of the smarties. You may be surprised that you actually have to *choose* a topic because you're just so incredibly multitalented!

Don't assume that different topics will damage your credibility. While Matt may only need to learn how to do spreadsheets, Geraldine may be thrilled to learn that you can also teach her how to read body language during sales meetings.

Sure, there's always a chance that somebody will claim to be an expert on a subject that he or she really knows nothing about, but that's the beauty of the "free" class. No one's losing any money and legally, it's nothing more than friends offering friends advice. This is an important understanding in your smarties group. After all, you don't want Geraldine suing when her inability to follow through on your "Getting the Money You Deserve" workshop lands her in the unemployment line.

✆ ﾉpeaking of ﾉmartieﾉ ...

Check out some of these groundbreaking women:

- In 1762, Ann Franklin became the first woman to hold the title of newspaper editor (at the *Newport Mercury* in Newport, Rhode Island).
- In 1849, Elizabeth Blackwell became the first woman to receive a medical degree in the United States (from the Medical Institution of Geneva, New York).

- In 1853, Antoinette Brown Blackwell became the first American woman ordained a minister by a recognized denomination (The First Congregational Church in South Butler, New York).
- In 1869, in the days before law school was a requirement to become a lawyer, Arabella Mansfield became the first female lawyer in the United States. A year later, Ada H. Kepley of Illinois graduated from the Union College of Law in Chicago. She was the first woman to graduate from a law school. (**Source:** corsinet.com/trivia/1-triv2.html)

36

The Future Is Now

Keep your eyes peeled to spot trends in your industry.

"Change is certain. Progress is not."
—E. H. Carr

Retro country fans will recall the Johnny Cash song "The Legend of John Henry's Hammer" about the railroad steel-driving laborer who loses his job and life to the steam drill that replaced him. Just think: if poor John had been savvy enough to spot trends in his industry, he could have saved himself a lot of sweating and calluses by investing in steam drills instead.

In industry, as in life, trends keep cycling and nothing hot stays hot forever. Yesterday's Rubik's Cube gives way to today's Playstation, and the once-zippy 32K modem now moves laughably slow. Want to practically guarantee you're always employable, and score points with the company higher-ups at the same time? Learn to spot trends in your industry and build a reputation as the office oracle.

How do you develop a sixth sense of what direction your business is going? By keeping your eyes peeled and drawing some well-thought conclusions from what you notice. For example, do you notice more and more temp/contract workers appearing in your department? Chances are your company only needs short-burst help, without the added costs of benefits and other perks. If it's part of your job, scope out temporary agencies that offer the most reliable help at the best prices. If you know of big projects coming down the pike, preempt the rush by arranging for temp help early.

Trend spotting is especially helpful in keeping you hot on the employment market. Make it a point to eyeball the job requirements of your dream position. Notice certain requirements that keep popping up in job descriptions, or a certain certification that's mentioned more and more? Get that experience and start reaping the results.

One great way to stay on top of the job market is to join a professional association. From bricklayers to hairdressers to female CFOs to Jell-O wrestlers, there's an organization that represents those in the profession, with cool perks like networking luncheons and magazines. Chat up some of your fellow workers and keep an eye out for tidbits that might be affecting you.

Trend spotting is crucial for those working outside corporate America, too. If you're involved in a company whose future is affected by politics, you might develop a whole new interest in who gets elected. Elections for city council reps and other officials elicit cheers and jeers from all sorts of people treading water while the ripple effect is going on. When an education-backing politico takes office, savvy teachers take notice.

Then there are the trends going on outside your specific industry. Your car salesman cousin complains that business is slower than ever. If the sagging economy has folks driving their cars longer than anticipated, they might be too strapped to patronize your restaurant and rack up a hefty tab for dinner and drinks. On the other hand, does everyone seem to be rolling in dough? Then go ahead—open that store that sells luxury fur-lined doohickeys and giddily anticipate soaring profits.

News junkies and other bookworms need look no further than the daily paper to get a dose of future possibilities. Everything from fluffy feature stories (Suede is out, vinyl's in? Guess you can cross suede cleaner off your list!) to hard business reports (Another corporate CEO busted . . . might people's mistrust of mega-conglomerates mean a boost for small businesses?) can hint at changes a-brewing on the business front.

37

And the Winner Is . . .

Attend your company's awards banquet to
support coworkers and gain motivation.

"To err is human, but it feels divine."
—**Mae West**

Here's a little test:
Your company is holding a big awards ceremony. You haven't
been nominated for anything. Do you:

A. Bag it. You don't owe the company anything and it's not
   required that you go.
B. Go to earn brownie points and snag some free food.
C. Go to support your coworkers, mingle with the execs, and learn
   more about your company.

Aha! Trick question! The answer is a fun and functional combination of B and C!

And just to clarify, earning brownie points doesn't have to mean
"sucking up." It could mean just showing your boss that you're a team
player (and a good sport if you *were* up for an award but lost).

Going to an awards ceremony doesn't have to be boring. It gives
you a chance to dress up, practice your table manners, meet people

from your company (and your company's clients), and perhaps even bust a move!

Supporting your coworkers also shows solidarity, support, and commitment to your company. What better way to squelch those rumors that you hate your job? Show up and show off—your intelligence, that is. You'll finally be able to put faces to all those names, and you may even get a few compliments.

"Oh! You're that lovely phone voice who always helps me get answers to my questions!"

Attending the awards banquet may also get you privy to information you might not otherwise learn at the office. We're not necessarily talking about overhearing private conversations, but rather just interpreting the awards ceremony and its recipients.

When Judy in human resources earns Company MVP, for example, it may help you realize that she really *is* working late all those nights—as opposed to having an affair with the janitor. (You should know better than to listen to the grapevine!)

And if the company earns an award for exceeding sales quotas (by millions!), it may be a hint that it's a good time to ask for that raise. Likewise, if the master of ceremonies takes the liberty of announcing that your boss is being transferred to London, it may accelerate your move to ask for a promotion. After all, he knows how hard you've worked for the past six years, right? You certainly don't want to wait *another* six while the new boss gets to know how wonderful you are.

On the downside, you may suddenly learn that Linda is going to be your new boss. Uh-oh. Maybe it's time you moved past that fight over the Hong Kong account.

Most important, attending an awards ceremony can make you feel like part of the team. It can remind you why you like your job so much and motivate you to do your best work. Maybe next year *you'll* be bringing home a trophy.

Fun Factoid

Here are just a few groundbreaking women who have paved the way for today's hip working chick:

- Lettie Pate Whitehead, 1934—first American woman to serve as a director of a major corporation, the Coca-Cola Company.
- Wallis Warfield Simpson, 1936—first *Time* magazine "Woman of the Year."
- Susanna M. Salter, 1887—first female mayor in the United States (Argonia, Kansas). She won by a two-thirds majority but didn't even know she was in the running until she went into the voting booth. Her name was submitted by the Women's Christian Temperance Union. She died at the age of 101 in 1961.

38

The Cradle Will Rock

Organize to balance work and kids without guilt.

"Trust yourself. You know more than you think you do."
—Dr. Benjamin Spock

Now that the kids are back in school, you've alphabetized the spice rack, hand made twenty-six different curtains for the living room, and elevated vacuuming to an art form. Face it honey, you are B-O-R-E-D! Not only that, but you're starting to notice businesswomen on the street and getting that jealous little glimmer in your eye . . . "I used to have a job," you pout. "Now I just have pudding in my hair."

Even if you're part of the lucky mommy minority that's been able to stay home with your young'uns, chances are you'll want to return to the workforce someday. When that someday comes, a few pointers are necessary to keep you from flipping out or feeling like the Worst Mother in the Whole World for returning to work.

Many moms who've returned to work swear that staying organized is the key to making a smooth transition. If you don't already have one, post a giant wipe-off scheduling calendar on the refrigerator to keep track of the schedule of everyone in the household, and copy the information in your Day-Timer as well. Keeping one master schedule is crucial when balancing soccer games, karate practice, and school-related meetings with your own business appointments. If you have a husband or partner in the house, assign him kid duty a few days a week, to keep yourself from getting overwhelmed. If you're like most women, you already take on too much in an effort to be Super-woman—surely your man can help out by offering to escort the "fruit of his loins" to the bus stop.

Another trick of the working mom trade is getting ready for the morning rush during the evening before. Have a nine-year-old daughter who takes forty-five minutes to pick something to wear? Have her lay her school outfit out the night before. This helps prevent you from feeling like spitting tacks when you're late for an early morning meeting because your little Kelsey couldn't decide between the pink sparkly or the green sparkly shirt. Prepacking lunches is another great way to cut down the number of steps in your morning household routine.

Never underestimate the boon of cool kitchen gadgets that help, too. Things as simple as a self-starting coffee pot, stocking up on quickie cereals that kids can serve themselves, and grab-and-go snacks that can be munched in the car add up to shave five or ten whole minutes off your morning "go time."

Check This Out, Mom

Families with married moms and dads who both work are the majority. Families where Dad's the breadwinner represent under 25 percent of families these days. According to census statistics, about 59 percent of moms returned to the workforce within a year after having a baby.

39

Buns of Steel

Do the ultimate desk butt crunch!

> "Three o'clock is always too late or too early
> for anything you want to do."
> —Jean-Paul Sartre

To unsuspecting coworkers, you're sitting at your desk typing at the speed of light to finish the end-of-week report. You're focused, engrossed, and looking intense. Little do they know that you're secretly tightening your butt muscles on the company's time.

No, it's not that bran muffin you had for breakfast trying to make a run for it. It's the ultimate desk butt crunch! That's right, for this low introductory price of—*nothing*—you, too, can have a tight derriere!

Unlike the costly machines or embarrassment that comes along with spandex at the gym, clenching your butt muscles in the privacy of your own office chair is not only free, but discreet. No one knows you're flexing while you're filing and you're killing two birds with one stone, which is not only efficient, but empowering. The cost-effective use of time will help you move down your to-do list quickly, saving more time for the important things in life—like shoe shopping or people watching, which require a serious commitment to time at the mall.

Seriously, who has time to head to the gym after work? By the time you head home to let your retriever out and grab a bite to eat, it's time for "Alias" or "CSI." No one in her right mind would try to motivate herself to change into workout clothes and drive across town to voluntarily strap into a modernized torture apparatus.

On the off chance that someone does inquire as to your sudden repetitive heightening, you will have to decide whether or not to share your exercise routine. As a rule of thumb, use these guidelines:

* **Good friend:** Share your knowledge. She'll be grateful and may say something flattering like, "I *knew* your butt looked better than ever!"
* **Casual acquaintance:** Vaguely share your knowledge, sensing for judgment as you explain. A candid interest may indicate that further information is safe to share.
* **Office pervert or gossip:** Lie. Explain that OSHA requires you to perform a variety of seated exercises daily in order to prevent work-related injuries. Start rolling your head to distract from the inquirer's memory of your butt clenches. Wiggle your fingers to imply anti–carpal tunnel syndrome strategies.

Oddly enough, you may find that someone else in your office is using your routine. It could be Jenny in engineering or Melissa on the fourth floor. The trick is to try to figure out who's been working "behind the scenes." You may want to check out the butt on Matt in operations. Call it research.

Speaking of sitting on your butt all day . . .

- An office chair with wheels will travel an average of eight miles a year.
- The World's Largest Office Chair is thirty-three feet tall.
- Miriam Benjamin received a patent for an invention she titled a "Gong and Signal Chair for Hotels." She was the second black woman to receive a patent.

40

Walk It Off

Change your scenery for fifteen minutes
and get a new perspective.

The phone won't stop ringing. The receptionist the temp agency sent keeps fiddling with her nose ring and accidentally hanging up on customers. If you have to hunt down one more misplaced file, you're gonna go off. To top it off, the combination of inane office Muzak and fluorescent lighting is starting to give you a whopping migraine.

Whoa, Nellie! Take a deep breath, push yourself back from your chair, and take a break. Remember the good old mandatory ten-minute break? For those of us accustomed to six-minute lunches at the desk and mandatory overtime, a break is what's otherwise known as a brief respite from work as a means of preserving sanity. In most states, anyone working six or more hours a day is entitled to a break—whether your company wants you to take it or not.

Getting out for a walk and staring at something besides a computer screen works wonders for your spirit and energy level. Corporate America won't cave if you take a ten-minute stroll around the block. In fact, the unrecirculated air and dose of sunshine may lend a well-needed boost to your internal energy source that'll make you even more productive when you return.

Whether you're toiling away in an office high-rise or slinging hash in a street corner diner, your break will be the most effective if you get out for a stroll. If you find yourself antsy and your brain dulled from sitting still too long, your bod's telling you, "Move around, already!" Even if your job's not sedentary, the increased oxygen intake and break from the work environment is a good thing.

Hate to exercise? That's yet another reason to take a stroll! Lazier lasses feel they have too much other stuff to do at night (lying comatose on the couch, inhaling popcorn in front of the TV, etc.) to take even a ten-second stroll, let alone a ten-minute one. But walking to escape work for a while feels like a whole different thing.

Your walk can whisk you even farther away from the working world if you remember to take headphones along. Unless chirping birds and babbling brooks dot the downtown landscape where you're strolling, you'll need to create your own sense of auditory pleasure . . . unless you find cars with no mufflers and blaring horns refreshing. Since the whole point of this is to break from your work environment, consider this your time to bask in sound waves you can't hear at your desk. Indulge your hankering for heavy metal riffs, a naughty comedy concert tape, or some bumpin' gangsta rap.

✂ Take a Walk, Already!

Did you know that taking just one ten-minute brisk stroll adds up? Hoofing it every workday can burn almost four hundred calories a week, more if the terrain is hilly. That's enough to earn a chunk of cheesecake each weekend, or shave off five pounds of fat per year.

41

StairMaster

Deliver everything yourself and slim those calves!

*"The only reason I would take up jogging is
so that I could hear heavy breathing again."*
—Erma Bombeck

Just because you *have* an elevator at work doesn't mean you have to use it! That's like saying that you had to eat the entire box of chocolates because your boyfriend gave them to you. (OK. Bad example. You *did* have to eat that entire box. Still, you get the point.)

Climbing the stairs to deliver packages, go to the bathroom, or attend a staff meeting can be a very invigorating experience. Not only will you get your blood pumping, which will help energize you, but you'll also start shaping your calves!

If your job includes answering phones or manning every second of the stock market's rises and falls, at least take two ten-minute breaks during the day when someone else can fill in for you. Find a set of stairs—even if there are only three steps—and do some walks up, down, and even sideways if you're coordinated. If you're in a one-floor building and only have one step, balance the balls of your feet on the stair and let your heels hang off the edge. Stretch up toward the sky, then relax and repeat. This will help build your calf muscles just as well—although it won't give you as good a cardio workout.

If you don't have a stair to work on, look for other "steps." A cement parking blockade or curb will work well if it's not a busy street (or right in front of your boss's window). And unless you want to be mistaken for a Peeping Tom, opt for someplace other than the curb in front of the clothing store next door.

There are advantages to delivering things yourself besides slimming your calves. You'll increase your visibility in the company; in both seeing what's going on and in being seen. Be sure to dress for success if you're going to power walk through the halls like you're on a mission to meet the boss. No one will be eager to promote "that frumpy girl who shuffles whenever she delivers stuff on this floor." Managers might, however, be willing to discuss a move for "that classy power suit–clad woman who takes the time to deliver everything in person."

Of course, after a few months, they may be describing you as "that hot VP with the nice calves from the corner office with a view."

Did you know . . .

When ballpoint pens were first sold in 1945 at Gimbels in New York City, five thousand people packed the store to get a chance to buy one. The cost? A mere $12.50. Fifty additional police officers were called in to control the crowds, and forty-seven people fainted in the crush. About ten thousand pens were sold in six hours, and an average of six thousand pens were sold daily for four months after that—despite the fact that the pens didn't work very well. (**Source:** http://vigilanteventures.com/trivia/office.htm)

42

Community Clothing

Start a career-clothes library and double your wardrobe.

"Good clothes open all doors."
—**Thomas Fuller**

From the plastic name tag on a fast-food uniform to the engraved leather briefcase, our clothes label us (quite literally, in the fast-food example). Whether you think panty hose are a curse of womanhood, or just can't stand to wear anything but jeans, business etiquette dictates that you dress the part, whatever the part may be. Smart chicks know that even if their favorite weekend look involves six-inch stilettos and a feather boa, their office look better be a tastefully tailored suit and sensible pumps if they want to get ahead.

Paying for all that attire is another matter entirely. Price dictates that the typical career woman's closet runs woefully heavy on beige Dockers and such (yawn!), while superstylish stuff is usually favored by the corner office type. Does that mean you have to set your credit card to the "kill, don't stun" setting to keep pace? Not by a long shot! Start a clothing exchange with like-minded and similarly sized buddies, and watch your career-wear options stretch faster than you can say "elastic waistband."

Unlike buying and selling on consignment where money is exchanged, a clothing exchange literally functions freely. Basically, it's trading stuff you don't wear any longer with other working women.

An exchange gets little-worn togs working for the group. Next time an item's too itchy, rides up, is the wrong color, or you're simply tired of wearing it, set it aside for the exchange. After all, why should a perfectly good suit languish in the back of your closet when it could be helping your cousin Suzie clinch a deal *and* earn your pal Pamela "best dressed" points at a job interview?

Saving money's the big boon, but saving time scores points for exchangers, too. Plenty of petite women, plus sizers, beanpoles, and other specialty-sized women dread poring over the specialty racks at the local mall only to find stuff in their size that they wouldn't be caught dead in. But trading items with a handful of girlfriends means that the more participants, the more fashion finds there are to choose from.

Friends too tiny, stingy, or poorly dressed to participate? Gather gals from built-in groups you already belong to that meet regularly (the gym, theater group, church, overeater's support group, etc.). Starting one is as simple as posting a note on the bulletin board or in a newsletter, or as informal as spreading the word. Have everyone bring her clean, unwanted items on a set day, and simply swap item for item with your similarly savvy sisters. Don't forget to include handbags and shoes, too, since there's less sizing and fitting to finagle.

Just as "never wash red socks with whites" is a universal laundry rule, setting some rules for the clothing exchange is smart. Clarify to all that a clothing exchange is not the same as lending/borrowing, which demands the item be returned. Agree that unless otherwise spelled out, once a tog is passed to another's hands, the original owner loses all rights to it. This should prevent any "hurry up and wear that blazer because I want it back for a big meeting" hassle. By the same token, the stuff should keep circulating to give all girls a chance to look fabulous. So, no hogging those snappy wool slacks that make your butt look a full size smaller!

43

Isometrics

Build muscles without the weight (or wait!).

"Back in my rummy days, I would tremble and shake for hours upon arising. It was the only exercise I got."
—W. C. Fields

Oddly enough, your boss isn't exactly thrilled by the idea of you going to the gym for three hours in the middle of the day. There are hundreds of calls to be made, thousands of clients to schmooze, and zillions of papers to be rifled through—all of which lead to the reasons you can't possibly head to the gym *after* work. (And don't anyone *dare* suggest a morning workout!)

Luckily, there are ways to burn calories and strengthen and tone muscles at the comfort of your own desk. Yes, we know about the butt crunches—but we're talking about the rest of the body: arms, legs, abs, and even back muscles. We're talking about isometrics.

You've probably heard the term but may not fully understand what it means or how the exercise works. Basically, it involves muscle contraction by pushing, pulling, or pressing against an immovable object. The beauty of isometrics is that it's nonstrenuous, convenient, and fast. Yeah, it sounds like a "get rich quick" scheme for exercise. But it's a proven form of exercise, and what do you have to lose? Here are a few isometric exercises to try at your desk while you're on the phone, using the computer, or just taking a break from the paperwork teepee that's formed on your desk.

Want to tone your inner thigh muscles? Place your wastepaper basket between your feet under your desk and squeeze. Hold for ten seconds and relax. Repeat. Just make sure the can isn't full or you could end up squeezing yesterday's lunch out onto the floor.

If you have a small enough desk, grab the outer edges and squeeze in hard for ten seconds. Repeat five times to tone the muscles of your upper chest.

No matter how big your desk, you can work your upper arm muscles by placing your palms slightly apart on your desk. Just press, relax, and repeat. You can do the same thing by placing your hands under your desk and pressing up.

Stuck in traffic? Don't panic. Use your time wisely by exercising your arm and upper chest muscles. Just place your hands at nine o'clock and three o'clock on the steering wheel (Your driver's ed instructor would be pissed! "It's ten and two! Ten and two!") and squeeze hard. To work your back muscles, push back against the seat instead. Hold and repeat.

Trying to tighten those stomach muscles before you have to fit in that slinky little dress next month? Here's one to do from your chair. Just stretch your arms out straight, place your palms on your thighs, and press down while you pull in your stomach muscles. Don't even try to pretend you don't know how to suck in your gut.

Last but not least, if you're stuck on an endless call, just lean to get lean! Stand arm's length from the wall and push your free hand's palm against it. Hold, relax, and repeat. Your conference call will never be the wiser.

44

Management Mutiny

Jump ship to another department without angering your current captain.

Some gals love the predictability of plodding away at the same job, year after year. Maybe it's the comfort found in knowing all the ins and outs of a certain job, or an inexplicable love of routine coupled with a resistance to change. "Only 8,352 more days," Rita Routine says. "Then I can retire with a giant pension and a gold watch!"

But what if your personality is more like Vicki Variety, who's always seeking new challenges on the employment horizon? What's more, what if you simply love the company you work for, and don't want to completely jump ship? Consider transferring to a new department or job within your existing company!

Chucking the job without chucking the whole company definitely has its advantages. On the surface, transferring departments offers all of the benefits (new responsibilities and opportunities to excel, possibly better pay and a fresh set of coworkers) with none of the drawbacks of starting a brand new job (adjusting to a new commute, interrupting health and other benefits, and decoding a new corporate culture, to name a few). With a little finesse, you can maneuver a move to greener pastures without starting a major brushfire in the process.

First, check your company's policy on transferring before you proceed. Some companies insist on workers staying in a position for a mere six months before thumbs-upping a major move, while others expect employees to slave away a full two years in one position before allowing a transfer. They want to retain the employee as a resource, but don't want to leave managers high and dry. If so, that pesky policy is all your current manager needs to veto a move, holding you back and leaving you sulking like a grounded teenager.

But if you're within the company guidelines, you're in business (no pun intended). Before announcing your intentions to your boss, get chummy with key members of the department you're considering joining. Volunteer for outside projects, join the softball league, cover open shifts—take this golden opportunity to find out what it's really like on their side of the fence. Any excuse to officially hang around and take note of red flags (tyrannical bosses, crabby coworkers, or mandatory overtime) may help you make up your mind. Doing so will give you a real view of life on another floor, and establish some key contacts if you decide to go for it.

Once you know there's a position open and you're ready to exit stage left, declare your intentions to your boss as soon as possible. Simply state that you feel you've gone as far as possible in your current position and are seeking another job within the company. Throw in some upbeat work-speak stuff, like saying you "truly value the experience you've gained working under your current boss and are certain he or she will support you as you seek further professional growth" for good measure to let your boss know you'd appreciate his or her seal of approval.

Organize a smooth departure, and you'll thank yourself later. After all, it's hard to negotiate your way to the top if you burn bridges along the way.

45

Where Do I Sign?

Look beyond the windfall to understand your signing bonus.

"No one can earn a million dollars honestly."
—**William Jennings Bryan**

"Oooh! A hefty sum of cash? Think of the bills I'll pay down, the wardrobe I can buy, the savings fund I can start. Where do I sign?"

Not so fast. Sure, a signing bonus is (as Martha Stewart says) "a good thing." Still, you need to know exactly what you're getting—and *not* getting. Go into your meeting educated, and you may be able to look past the lump sum long enough to understand all your options.

Here are a few questions to consider when being offered a signing bonus.

* **Will I still be eligible for performance bonuses?** Some companies offer a signing bonus in lieu of performance bonuses. If this is not the case, ask when you'll be eligible for your first performance bonus and how often you'll be reviewed (e.g., once per year). Be sure you're clear on how your performance bonuses are determined (e.g., sales goals or low turnover rate, depending on your position).

* **Is this bonus split, with part paid upon hire and part paid after a set time?** If your signing bonus is split, find out exactly when

you'll receive the remaining part of your bonus. Also, be clear on what percentage is received up front. You don't want to learn later that the company is only offering 10 percent up front and 30 percent after three-month increments.

* **Do I forfeit any or all of my bonus if I leave before a certain time period?** This is always a tough question because there may be concern on your part—and the part of the employer—that the question implies an intention to quit soon after hire. Still, it's a reasonable question. If you do forfeit some or all of your money, ask how much and what the time period is. It may help you make decisions if you do decide to leave. There's also a chance that you may have to pay the money back if you receive all of your bonus upon hire and then leave the company.

* **How much are other companies in this industry offering executives in my position with my experience?** This is more of a research question, as the employer may not know the answer to this question or just may be hesitant to answer. Check the Internet for employment sites that list average signing bonuses for your industry, position, and experience.

Many companies are now offering stock options in place of signing bonuses. This is especially true with start-up companies whose stocks have not gone public yet, the theory being that employees will take the chance that their stock shares will be worth more than a signing bonus once the company goes public.

The offer is certainly one to ponder, as some employees have literally "struck it rich" overnight. On the other hand, other companies' stock ends up worth little—leaving you with nothing gained and a signing bonus lost.

If you truly believe that taking the stock options may be a smart financial choice, do your research. When weighing the pros and cons of stock options, consider some of the following questions to determine possible factors in the value of company stock:

* Is the company growing or downsizing?
* Is the company the result of an acquisition or a planned expansion?
* Has the growth affected its profitability?
* What is the growth potential of the company's products or services?
* What is the company's market share?
* Who are its competitors?
* How do other employees feel about owning company stock?
* Have past employees chosen stock over signing bonuses?
* When does the company plan to go public (if not already)?
* What percentage of the company stock would you receive?

Of course, there are always other options. Why not ask for a split between cash and stocks? Or how about a smaller signing bonus in exchange for more frequent performance reviews?

If you're feeling uncomfortable with the offer, speak up. There's no harm in attempting to negotiate. After all, despite the employer's position behind the big desk and stack of résumés, *you're* the one holding all the cards—and the pen.

46

Recycle It!

Be kind to the earth—start an office recycling program.

> *"We have forgotten how to be good guests, how to walk lightly on the earth as its other creatures do."*
> —**Barbara Ward Jackson**

You're a diligent citizen of the earth. Maybe you even consider your-self a tree hugger. You rinse out and save those yucky tin cans and swish out your milk jugs, hoping they'll be reconstituted into a funky plastic chair someday.

It only makes sense that you'd recycle at your office, where you spend most of your day, right? Maybe not. It's hard to believe that here in the twenty-first century, a minority of American businesses have an active recycling program, and fewer still make a point of using recy-cled products. Make your Mother Earth proud and get your company on the recycling bandwagon!

But before you go to the maintenance and janitorial crew in a self-righteous, "we must recycle!" huff, check to see what's already being done to be earth-friendly. You may see coworkers carelessly tossing an occasional can out, but your company may be recycling much of its office paper without much fanfare.

The first point of business should be to get some recycling bins put into the kitchen. Even a simple plastic bin for aluminum cans and per-haps another for plastics would go a long way toward saving resources, and help your company score feel-good PR points, too. Should you recycle glass, too? It's a tough call: glass recycles well, but bins could be very heavy and shards could be dangerous. If you'll be the Good Samaritan who'll be delivering the collection to a recycling station, think twice.

If you have a maintenance crew that will be handling the bins, you'll only be collecting kudos for a good idea. If it's a small office and you'll be implementing recycling yourself, get bright plastic bins that won't be mistaken for trash, and be sure to put laminated signs on each bin with the rules, e.g., "Aluminum Cans Only," big enough to banish trash. Nothing's grosser than scoring a booty of cans, only to find them covered with coffee grounds and watermelon rinds.

The next order of business is what to do with all this recycling. Set a schedule (every two weeks or so) to bundle papers and place cans in a bag. To remove your recycling, the easiest option is to put it out with the regular office garbage. Ask the janitorial staff where the garbage goes out, and call the garbage company's customer service number to inquire about office recycling pickup. If not, look up "recycling" in the yellow pages and find a center that offers pickup service. Remember that pickup fees might cut into any aluminum can profits you might have hoped to collect for the company Christmas party.

Next, it's on to the copier. Some offices are progressive enough to set all printers to double-sided print, which only makes sense. Think about it: if the literary masterpieces of the world are printed in books double sided, surely your company's boring quarterly reports can be printed double sided, resulting in a huge cutback in the amount of paper you use. Buy 100 percent recycled paper to complete the cycle. If the boss balks at the lack of whiteness or slightly higher cost of 100 percent recycled, point out that the recycle symbol will look good for the company. Or, use the bleached and toxic-but-pretty stuff for official correspondence, saving the recycled stuff for everyday business purposes. Setting your print quality from high to normal can save a toner cartridge or two per year per printer, with only a slight change in print quality.

Finally, what to do with all that potentially damaging and highly confidential information once it's shredded? Why, recycle the paper shreddings, of course! Stationery, toilet paper, cardboard boxes . . . you name it, it probably contains paper shreddings. Be sure your paper shredder is the crosscut kind, and find out from your recycling company what form it can take shreds in. You might have to "recycle" it by talking the mailroom into using shreddings as box padding, rather than fabricated plastic bubble wrap or those annoying Styrofoam thingies.

47

Cracking the Whip

Apply the Golden Rule and
discipline subordinates appropriately.

> *"Be nice to people on your way up
> because you meet them on your way down."*
> **—Jimmy Durante**

Unless you own the company, there will always be a chance that someone will have to discipline you someday. Take that into consideration under the biblical phrase "Do unto others as you would have them do to you."

If this is your first time acting as the wicked stepmother, use the following general guidelines when disciplining a subordinate.

Get all the facts. Before you can determine a punishment (or just a finger-wagging), learn the truth about what happened. If this means calling in witnesses, do so in a private setting. Think of it as a court proceeding: "Innocent until proven guilty." Invite the parties into your office or a meeting room and allow each side to speak in front of the other. If each party is brought in separately, they may be more likely to stretch the truth.

Make sure the punishment fits the crime. If there aren't specific guidelines written up in an employee manual (e.g., stealing staplers is cause for termination), consider the weight of the offense. Perhaps John just drank Laura's milk because he thought it was his. Or maybe she took on his client because her supervisor told her to while John was on vacation.

Also, consider the employee's record and job performance. Is he a repeat offender, frequently accused of bad-mouthing other employees to clients? Does she often "forget" receipts or have unexplained purchases on her company credit card?

Many companies offer verbal or written warnings for first-time offenses. Be sure to check the employee's record for previous offenses.

Use the proper procedures and verbiage. As with any perpetrator, anything the person says can and will be used against him or her. The same goes for you as the employee's boss.

Once you've determined the facts, be sure that the employee is aware of not only why his or her actions were wrong, but what will happen if he or she does it again.

Explain why the company enforces such rules without raising your voice or sounding accusatory or condescending. If you can determine that the intention was not to do wrong, reassure the employee that you're not accusing him or her of causing intentional harm. "Paul, I understand that your intention was not to harm the company, but it's important that we honor our clients' confidentiality agreements in order to maintain trust and integrity. I understand that this was simply a mistake and I'm sure it won't happen again."

If the offense requires that you fire the employee, ask your boss to be present in the room to decrease the chances of a lawsuit or violent response.

Some companies allow employees to resign rather than being fired. Discuss your options with your superior and/or the director of human resources before putting the offer to resign on the table.

48

Parting Ways

Know when it's time to go.

> *"When you cease to make a contribution, you begin to die."*
> —**Eleanor Roosevelt**

It's Sunday evening. You start to get that awful feeling in the pit of your stomach, knowing tomorrow is yet another Monday at that dark, depressing salt mine called work.

You didn't always feel this way about your job. In fact, you started out bright eyed, brimming with fresh ideas and always arrived five minutes early. Now you're practically persecuted daily, those fresh ideas are now stale, and your attitude has totally tanked.

Is it time to change jobs?

Working women are faced with this daunting question a number of times in our lives. Every time we quit one venture to undertake another, we're unwittingly making several tiny judgment calls in our quest to ditch drudgery in search of greener pastures. Are we just reacting to a bad week? Do we just need a vacation, promotion, or a transfer to another department? Would quitting the current job be the ticket to a prosperous future, or would it be cutting off your nose to spite your financial face?

Before you tender a resignation you may regret, consider the following issues:

* **Time invested.** Career experts bicker about the length of time it takes to adjust to a new job. If you've been on the job three months or less, chances are you may just be experiencing new-job jitters. Perhaps your opinion of the job will change once you know the ropes. Choose a date thirty days out, and mark it on your calendar. Then agree to give the new job your all and suspend judgment until that day. Meanwhile, keep a "job journal" (in a secret place, of course) and record your innermost thoughts during the time to chart your feelings. If after thirty days it still feels sucky, that may make up your mind for you.

* **New job, or new career?** If you enjoy aspects of your job but hate the work environment, perhaps the same job at a new place is in order. But if the job's daily tasks leave you saying to yourself, "Ugh! How did I end up doing X when my dream is to do Y?" and plenty of your day is spent daydreaming about winning the lottery, a career overhaul may be in order. Get some career testing, read career books, and start pinpointing what you really want to do with your life. Invest time in your career search now, and the next job you accept could be the job of your dreams.

* **What I like about you . . .** Perhaps your position needs a tune-up, rather than a complete overhaul. Determine what exactly it is that you find intolerable—then you'll know what to focus on. Is a crabby office mate or slave-driver boss tainting your whole view? Maybe a heart-to-heart chat with the boss or a request that your cubicle be moved elsewhere is in order. Does a hellish commute have you considering a job closer to home? Ask to alter your schedule, or stagger your hours to arrive later and leave later. Bored with your current duties? Propose a new project to your boss (and look like a go-getter besides!). If the job's a good fit after some tweaking, by all means stay. If all the tweaking in the world can't change the view, consider leaving.

Disliking your job for too long can make you feel powerless and woebegone—not a good place to be. The key is to take all points into consideration *before* switching jobs. Sometimes a job just doesn't work out, but at least you'll know you gave it your all before giving it the heave-ho.

49

Working Out the Kinks

Go to the gym and blast some stress away.

With the exception of beating the crap out of someone, there's nothing better to get out your aggression than heading to the gym. And since no one in your office is exactly volunteering to be your punching bag, you may as well take a little break.

If you're one of the lucky few who have a gym in your office building, you have no excuse. As long as there's a shower to ward off any post-workout stink, knock yourself out (so to speak) at lunch. Not only will it increase your energy for the rest of the day, but it will probably help you sleep better.

Another latent consequence of getting into a regular fitness routine is that it tends to decrease your appetite, or at the very least, you'll be more likely to reach for something healthy. When was the last time you left a gym and drove straight to McDonald's? It's like running a marathon and lighting up a cigarette as you cross the finish line.

If you don't have a gym in your office building or down the street, you'll have the option of going before or after work. Both have their advantages and disadvantages.

The morning routine will most likely be extremely difficult if you're a late-night person. On the other hand, it'll be a great start to your day. You'll feel energized and know that you can go straight home after work to enjoy your evening without the hassle of having to plan out a block of time for the gym.

Which leads us to the evening workout.

Heading to the gym after a long day at the office is often met with detours—to a restaurant, the grocery store, the video store, or a friend's house. The only thing more difficult than heading straight to the gym from work is trying to go home, walk your dog, check your E-mail, cook dinner, answer your phone calls, and sort through your mail before getting dressed in your sweats and heading *back* out to the gym.

So why would anyone bother? We're back to the aggression release. Running, kicking a bag, swimming, and even weight lifting can be a tremendous release to your body. Just imagine the huge report that's due tacked to the punching bag, or that the World's Worst Client you dealt with for five hours straight is chasing you from one end of the pool to the other.

Focus on the burn—knowing you're melting off calories, toning your body, and generally becoming a healthier, stronger woman for it. You'll be glad you did it (at least *after* it's over) and maybe you can treat yourself with (yet another) little black dress. After all, much like dates, you can't have too many.

50

Ants in Your Pants

Bring a blanket and goodies and
have a lunchtime picnic in the park.

"Earth laughs in flowers."
—**Ralph Waldo Emerson**

Unless you're a greenhouse employee or a manager who's scored a nifty corner office with giant windows that actually open, chances are you're shut off from the natural world from nine to five.

When lunchtime rolls around, most of us are just itching to get up and get out. So why on earth do so many of us get right back in our stuffy little cars and wait in line for fast-food schlock? Pack a picnic lunch and go to a nearby park to treat yourself to a leisurely lunch in the shade!

Even a humble little picnic can mean maximum relaxation if you remember to plan ahead. If you're feeling especially type A, go all out with linen napkins, a Brie wheel, grapes, and a tiny dessert tucked into a cute little picnic basket. Just remember to either choose stuff that keeps well in your car, or keep it in a nondescript grocery bag in the office fridge. You could bring the whole darn basket in, but brace yourself for a little good-natured "a tisket, a tasket" teasing from your work buddies.

It's easy to find a spot, even if you're in the city. There are plenty of little parks in each city neighborhood. Look at the phone book's city map around where you work. Chances are there's one a few blocks away that you didn't even know existed. No park? No problem. Plenty of office building complexes have lawns or landscape areas they've prettied up for employees to enjoy that you can park your picnic on. Don't be shy, it's open space! You don't have to work in a particular office building to soak up soda and sunshine on its sprawling lawn, either. Who's gonna bother a working girl on her much-deserved lunch break?

Too much trouble to pack all that stuff? Just chuck a jar of peanuts and a few pieces of fruit in the bottom of your tote bag. When it's picnic time, grab a cold pop out of the machine on your way out, and you're all set. Pack your headphones, and don't forget a beach blanket or ratty towel to sprawl out on sans shoes. A trashy novel and artist's sketchpad or stationery to jot stuff on takes picnicking to the mini-vacation level.

If you're a working mom, a midday picnic is perfect for reconnecting with your kids or capitalizing on some free midday minutes. If your workplace offers on-site day care, grab the kids and take advantage of lunch as a time to swing on the swing set and snack in the sunshine. If your babies are in school or at day care across town, plan a picnic with a friend to get some girlfriend face time without cutting into precious family time.

Think ahead and bring a tennis ball and racket and bat a few balls around. The worst tennis game ever still beats choking down a ramen noodle cup in your dingy cubicle, with your boss popping her head in every six minutes to say, "Oh, you're eating lunch . . . Here, let me just give you this one more thing . . ." If you're *at* lunch rather than simply *eating* lunch, your boss won't bug you midbite.

Just think: while your "eat at their desk" office mates will be pallid and spent halfway through the day, you'll breeze in as refreshed and recharged as if you just spent a weekend at the beach. Your job might be no picnic, but there's no rule that says your lunch hour can't be.

51

The Day-Care Dilemma

Trust your instincts to make wise decisions about child care.

> *"I am not young enough to know everything."*
> —Oscar Wilde

For women working outside the home, coping with career, financial, and possibly marital pressures is hard enough. Factor in day care for the working *mom*, and you have a whole new list of things to worry about.

As tough as finding good day care is, there's good news. First, choosing a child-care provider—be it an au pair, a neighbor, a preschool, or a day-care facility—means you can go back to work. This option is more than most women in the world have.

Second, no decision has to be final. Picking a child-care provider today doesn't have to lock you into a decision for good. If your needs or those of your child change, so can your provider. With this in mind, you can start to narrow down your options based on the following three criteria.

1. **Your child(ren)'s needs.** If you have more than one child, is it important that they be in the same program? If so, this may significantly cut down on your options, especially if their ages are greatly varied. Do your children have any special physical needs, such as dietary requirements or wheelchair accessibility?

You will also need to evaluate your children's developmental levels in order to seek an appropriate program to enhance their learning. Do your children have special developmental or educational needs—e.g., dyslexia or attention deficit hyperactivity disorder? If your children are exceptionally gifted, what type of program will keep them mentally stimulated and challenged?

2. **Your schedule.** "No problem. I'm a nine-to-fiver." Yeah, right. Remember that time last month when you had to go in at 6 A.M. four days in a row? Or that time last week when you got stuck in that meeting till 8 P.M.? And what about those power dinners, company functions, and end-of-the-month weekends when you're trying to get those papers ready for that big account? You may be *scheduled* to work nine to five, but you're nowhere near forty hours.

It's important to be realistic about your schedule. First, choose the basic hours that you'll need child care. Next, consider the location of the facility. How close is it to your home? To your work? Sure, something halfway between work and home sounds good, but if your partner works in the opposite direction from you, it may be better to have something close to your house if you're not the only one dropping off or picking up the kids.

You'll also need to consider the facility's extended hours in case you and/or your partner get stuck at work. (Or just want a night on the town!) If the facility closes at 6 P.M. and you get stuck in traffic, do you have a backup plan? The last thing you want to deal with is an angry provider who's been waiting with your kids for two hours *after* closing.

3. **Your budget.** This may seem obvious, but there's more than just the hourly or weekly fee involved. You'll need to include in your considerations gas, lunches and snacks for your children (if not included in the fees), whether you get income tax credits, charges if you pick up your children late, additional fees for nights, weekends, and holi-

days, application fees and deposits, and penalties (if any) for removing your children from the facility before the contract runs out.

Remember that, like many things in life, you get what you pay for. A less expensive program or provider may be cheaper for a reason. You'll need to ask yourself if you're willing to pay more for a better provider-to-child ratio, more flexible hours, a better location, or a more intensive learning/activities program.

No matter what type of child care you choose, be sure to evaluate your children's progress, health, and happiness on a regular basis. If your children are old enough, talk to them about what happens when you're at work. Are they happy? Are they eager to tell you about their experiences, accomplishments, and friendships? Do they appear to like their provider(s)? How do they react when you leave for the day? When you return for the day?

It's normal for children to need time to adjust to new surroundings, providers, and other kids. If they're still having difficulty after the first few weeks, however, you may need to reconsider the type of care you've chosen. When in doubt, remember the golden rule: follow your instincts. If you think you've chosen the wrong facility or type of care, keep looking. When you find the right provider, you'll know it.

52

Leaving on a Jet Plane

Bring travel brochures and start planning a team getaway.

> *"I travel not to go anywhere but to go. I travel for travel's sake.*
> *The great affair is to move."*
> **—Robert Louis Stevenson**

Are you and your coworkers beginning to feel like inmates in pantyhose prison, imprisoned within gray cubicle walls? Is your boss starting to resemble a maximum-security warden who harangues others with endless tasks and demands? Maybe it's time to start plotting a team-building breakout where fun and freedom reign and happy coworkers feel like your costars on "Gilligan's Island."

Whether you're planning a team day-trip or a working retreat for the entire department, traveling with coworkers has its advantages. Getting out of the office to work together helps you get to know your fellow staff members in a whole new light. What's more, the group activities and planned exercises that sound cheesy in the brochure may actually help you bond more cohesively with your office mates.

During your next commute, keep your eyes peeled for travel agencies, scuba shops, outdoor equipment providers, or other such businesses that are on the way. That dingy strip mall you cruise right past on the way to the office may have a kick-butt travel agency tucked away in the corner that specializes in groups. So many people plan trips over the Internet they forget what a fabulous resource their local travel agent can be. Pop into your local travel agent and ask what options are available for a company retreat. Any agent worth his or her salt will be happy to chat with you about package deals and corporate billing options.

Besides agents, scuba shops, and outdoor outfitters sometimes sponsor and plan related excursions that fit their customer niche. If a few coworkers share a love of hiking or the outdoors, you might want to get a deal at a mountain condo complex that offers both nearby trails and conference rooms for daytime meetings. Likewise with a beach-side resort, if most of your office mates are ocean fans.

Still need to plan, but feeling too lazy to leave the office? No problem! Shut your office door for a few moments and surf through the slew of travel-related websites. Reduced plane tickets, cozy chateaus, adventure dude ranches, and more await the savvy surfer. Thanks to the screamin'-fast Internet connections found at most businesses, you'll surf in the fast lane. Before you make any definite arrangements, check with coworkers to see if spouses, friends, or significant others will be tagging along for the retreat.

Check first whether or not your company monitors employee Internet access, or get your boss's permission to surf such sites. Some companies are very picky about which sites employees view during work hours. Beware of going off on a tangent while you're researching potential retreat travel plans. Do you really want your boss knowing you spent forty-seven minutes surfing nudistresorts.com when you were supposed to be comparison shopping hotels?

By using some downtime at work to plan a retreat, you'll save your free time for tackling other important issues . . . like ensuring you choose a condo with minibars in each room.

We've Come a Long Way, Baby

During World War II, more than six million women took over working in many fields for men who had been drafted. In 1944, the average woman's salary was $31.21 a week.

53

Your Cheatin' Heart

Schedule job interviews on your lunch hour.

"Some of us are becoming the men we wanted to marry."
—Gloria Steinem

Despite the word *lunch*, your lunch hour is yours to do with it what you will. If you want to run home and watch television, or take a dance lesson, that's your business.

That said, you're free to line up lunch-hour job interviews. After all, it's much more of a slap in the face to your boss if you actually take time *off* from work (i.e., come in late or leave early) to get in line with the competition. At least this way you're doing it on your time—and not putting your interviewer in a bad mood by making him or her stay after 5 P.M. to interview you on *your* schedule.

There are no doubt problems, however, when you're trying to squeeze an interview into a lunch hour, mainly, the time constraints. Unless the company you're aiming for is right down the street, you could spend twenty minutes driving there and twenty minutes driving back, leaving yourself only twenty minutes to be interviewed. This may be OK if you're applying for a manufacturing gig or to be a phone operator where your skills and experience from your résumé speak for themselves. If, however, you're applying for a gig as the vice president of foreign trade relations, you're better off scheduling a long dinner interview.

To remedy the problem, your best bet is to politely inform the interviewer of your time restrictions in advance. "Thank you for calling. Yes, I'd be very interested in coming in for an interview. In order to be respectful to my employer, I'd like to request a lunch-hour interview if possible. I have sixty minutes for lunch and with driving time, that can probably allow for a forty-five-minute interview. Is this a possibility?" If the person who calls you agrees, be sure to ask if he or she will be the one interviewing you. If not, be sure to request that the interviewer be told of your time constraints beforehand. You may even want to offer a gentle reminder when you arrive for the interview. Most people will be understanding if you explain that you're trying to be respectful of your current employer. Think of it like giving two weeks notice. Your interviewer will most likely appreciate that you're a courteous and respectful businesswoman.

Your other problem may be with your references. Be sure to note on your résumé that your current employer should *not* be contacted (unless your company is encouraging you to find another job due to upcoming layoffs) or you could end up without any job at all. Ditto with coworkers or friends with big mouths. If you list your friend Stacey as a reference, don't forget that she's dating Dan, and Dan's sister works at your company. Word travels just as fast with well-meaning friends who know not what they say in the heat of passion.

☏ Speaking of looking for another job . . .

- Only one out of every ten people surveyed say that they are satisfied with their jobs.
- It's estimated that 10 percent of résumés contain a fabricated job or college.

54

Green with Envy

Choose a positive response when a
coworker gets promoted.

*"Far and away the best prize that life offers
is the chance to work hard at work worth doing."*
—**Theodore Roosevelt**

You volunteered to take on extra work when your boss requested it. You busted your butt to do over and above what your position demands, and got a great performance review. You struggled and toiled in hopes that your extra efforts would pay off by landing you a plum promotion within the company once an opening occurred.

Then you heard through the office grapevine that Ms. So-and-So in your department is lobbying for the same position . . . and she has an advanced degree and more experience to boot! You both do your darnedest to cinch the interview, but when the news rolls in, it's not good. After looking at your skills and qualifications side by side, Ms. So-and-So was indeed promoted over you.

Plenty of less professional lasses would use getting bumped from the line waiting for a promotion as an excuse to find fault with upper managers and be grumpy in general. Not you, though. Why? Because you know that maintaining your current high standards and learning how to win the promotion next time virtually guarantee you'll get it next time.

At the first available opportunity, ask your manager to sit down with you and explain the areas where you fell short. By saying you want to be sure you're in the running for next time and wish to beef up your skills and qualifications, you're essentially saying, "Hey, I am a serious player, and am willing to hustle to get ahead." Managers universally love tenacity and a positive attitude, just as much as they universally hate whining and employees who pout when they don't get what they think they had coming to them. Once you know the areas where you're deficient, show 'em what you've got by taking initiative and having it covered next time. Your boss will likely be scoping you out extra critically to see how you handle this test—don't flunk it by losing steam or developing a chip on your shoulder.

Next, study the winner for clues on how to improve your own performance. Does she dress more professionally than you do? Is she more involved in extracurricular work projects within the company? How does she interact with her coworkers and superiors? Check her out—not to be a copycat, but to scope her out for critical details on how to improve your own performance. If you're on a semifriendly basis with her, tell her you'd love to check out her résumé. Then scour it to see how her education stacks up, what format she presents her information in, what paper it's printed on, what professional organizations she belongs to . . . everything. Learning more about her may illuminate a thing or two about yourself and where you're at professionally— "Hmmm, I *knew* I shouldn't have printed my résumé and references on bubblegum pink paper!"

Finally, just sit back and bide your time. Maybe the department will expand, creating all sorts of new jobs for positive and perky workers— meaning you!

Above all, keep your chin up and remember that good things come to those who wait—and who print their résumé on traditional white or beige paper, rather than bubblegum pink.

55

Sheepless in Seattle

Look perky after a restless night—or better yet,
cure your insomnia.

> *"The average, healthy, well-adjusted adult gets up
> at 7:30 in the morning feeling just plain awful."*
> —Jean Kerr

So you've had your third straight night of insomnia and are thinking about skipping work. Think again.

It's a busy day at the office and not one you could blow off without
(1) losing your job; (2) losing your best client; or (3) losing your mind
trying to play catch-up next week.

Your best bet is to put your makeover magic skills to work on those
dark circles under your eyes and get your mind set on the fact that
today *is* a workday.

First things first: take a shower. Chances are that if you've had very
little sleep, you're running late. But a shower is a much-needed indul-
gence. A little cold water at the end will perk you up and leave you
feeling refreshed.

Next, attend to the eyes. You'll need a bottle of eyedrops and slices
of cold cucumbers for the puffiness. Yes, a steak will work, too.

In addition to your appearance, you'll need to boost your energy
level. Caffeine (in coffee, tea, or soda) works temporarily but may leave
you dragging later in the morning when the effects wear off. Instead,

opt for some fruit juice (not fruit "drink," which is loaded with sugar), hot decaf tea, or if you just *have* to have your coffee—one cup with half regular and half decaf. A protein shake or fruit smoothie will also give you the much-needed vitamins and minerals for a longer boost of energy.

You'll also need protein and carbs for all-day sustenance. Peanut butter and crackers would be best, but work with what you have. (No, Reese's peanut butter cups don't count for protein.) Oatmeal or yogurt with fresh fruit will also give you a good start to your day, as will an egg with a whole-grain bagel or toast. The market is bursting with "energy" bars. Your best bet is something with less than two hundred calories and six grams of fat to get your protein and carbs without adding to your waistline.

This probably won't be the last time you have insomnia, so you may want to prepare for "next time" (which could be tonight!) just in case. Here are a few ideas to help you not only get more sleep, but survive the next day at work if you don't:

* Avoid caffeine after noon. Even decaf has some caffeine. Opt instead for juice, warm milk, a milk shake, or naturally decaffeinated tea.
* Go to bed earlier than usual and take a favorite book, some soothing music, or a meditation audio book.
* Dim the lights. Begin turning the lights down or off early in the evening. Draw the shades if you have streetlights that shine in your window.
* Plan your next day before you go to bed. Make your to-do list, iron your clothes, set the table for breakfast—whatever it takes to give your mind a rest.
* Take sleeping pills only if you can get a full eight hours of rest. Any less could leave you feeling groggy or disoriented the next morning.

* Stick to a routine. Your body craves routine to stay balanced. Go to bed at the same time every night and wake up at the same time—even if you're tired. Eating meals at the same time every day can also help regulate your body.

* Get regular exercise. Studies show that people who exercise regularly tend to sleep better.

* Use aromatherapy. Scents like lavender can help you unwind after work or relax before falling asleep. Avoid using candles unless someone else is around to blow them out if you fall asleep. Instead, opt for a scented bath, bead pillow, or lotion.

* Avoid using your bed for anything other than reading, sleeping, or sex. Your mind will begin to associate your bed with paying bills, watching television, or working on the laptop if you're not careful.

So what are you waiting for? Face the day with your best miracle yet—and hurry—before you know it, the day will be over and you'll be back in your own bed. Just make sure you unplug your phone. No sense putting yourself in the way of temptation if Mr. Right calls to say he's only in town for one night. At this point, you'd rather be dreaming about him anyway.

Recommended CDs:

* *Sleep Soundly* by Steven Halpern
* *Delta Sleep System* by Dr. Jeffrey Thompson

56

Simply Brilliant!

Pitch a new business idea to show off your initiative.

"Nothing happens unless first a dream."
—Carl Sandburg

From paper clips to Post-it Notes to childproof pill bottles, all of life's neatest inventions started with a simple idea.

Whether you're a lowest-rung-on-the-ladder secretary at your company or the CEO of a major conglomerate, generating brilliant business ideas is one of the surest ways to ensure your employability for a long time to come. Not only that, but if an idea of yours gets put into place and ends up to be a successful venture for your company, you could wind up with a plateful of new, exciting responsibilities, prestige among your peers, and a cushy corner office—good-bye lowest-rung-on-the-ladder position!

First things first, though. How does one generate brilliant business ideas? By paying attention and staying aware of the needs of your business, then brainstorming for new, creative ways to meet those needs. Not all ideas have to be far-out and "who'd have thought?" kooky to be successful, either. Some ideas are brilliant in their simplicity.

For example, let's say you work for a small custom-made furniture store. The owner is a whiz at designing chairs, but she's a low-tech type who's still lagging behind at getting the store online. What she may not realize is how creating a website will help her keep pace with her competitors, and how easy it may be to sell merchandise from the site. Being low-tech, she's probably intimidated by the whole concept of the Internet—but you're a World Wide Web wonder. Why not contact a few Web designers, collect a few estimates on website design, and present them to her as a potential new marketing venture? Present it confidently enough, and she may even let you spearhead the project!

If you're not a creative genius, don't fret. You can generate new business ideas simply by chatting with other members of your department about their needs or gripes. Do the salespeople in your company crab about wasting time calling on customers who aren't really interested? ("I can't believe I drove an hour to meet them, hoping to ink a deal, and all they wanted was the free promotional mouse pad!") Then maybe someone (namely you!) should place a prescreen phone call to potential clients to chat up the product, gauge their interest, and help generate buzz, for a small portion of the commission. The sales staff saves time by not calling on uninterested customers, and you get a cut for your effort. It's a win-win deal!

Don't pooh-pooh a potential idea because it's not your job, or you don't want to create extra work for yourself. Bosses love initiative, and whether a new idea's responsibilities would fall to you or not, you'll score kudos for its conception. To flesh out potential ideas, do some preliminary research online to see if other companies currently have your idea in place, and find out if it works for them. If your idea is costly, it might be a good idea to gather ballpark prices to include in your pitch. "How much will that cost?" is likely the first phrase your boss will utter—after praising your moxie, that is.

Whatever you do, don't dismiss a potentially great idea as unworkable or too far out before considering it closely first. After all, where would we be if the inventor of Post-it Notes had said to himself, "Sticky notes? Nah . . . Who'd ever buy such a thing?"

57

The Little Car That Couldn't

Deal with car problems.

"Is fuel efficiency really what we need most desperately? I say that what we really need is a car that can be shot when it breaks down."
—Russell Baker

After seventeen "car problems" in one year, it's amazing you still have a job. Unless your boss had a shabby beater himself once, it's impossible to understand why *he* hasn't sued your mechanic for your lost wages.

The most important thing you can do if you own a problematic car is to have a backup plan: a friend you can call for a ride, the bus schedule and nearest bus stop, or enough fare to catch the train, subway, or taxi. The last thing you need is to get fired for calling in because you can't get to work. Not to mention, you don't exactly have a plush enough savings account to pay for the cost of the repair *and* look for a new job.

If you never call in sick, you may get some sympathy from your coworkers because of your car-related absences. One may even offer to come to your house to follow you to the mechanic's just in case—or at the very least, offer you a ride to work once you get there. Take your coworker up on the offer or you'll be wishing you had when your car breaks down in the middle of traffic and you realize you've left your cell phone at home.

If it's a minor problem and your car can be fixed while you wait, be sure to call your boss again from the auto shop so she doesn't think you're just hung over from last night's Snoop Doggie Dog concert. Make sure there's plenty of clanking going on in the background when you call—it will lend credibility to your location.

Unfortunately, there's a chance that being late for work is going to be the least of your problems. Once you get the estimate for your repairs, you may miss a few more days of work due to the concussion you receive from your head making contact with the mechanic's waiting-room floor as you faint. Weigh the costs carefully. If you think there's a chance you have a lemon, you may want to just save the money and invest in a better car. No sense dumping $2,000 into a 1976 Datsun (no, it's not automatically a classic just because it's twenty-five years old) when you could put the money down on a newer car that doesn't require rolling down the window to open the door from the outside. Besides, think of all the money you'll save on insurance if you get a car with brakes.

58

Padding Your Nest Egg

Bone up on retirement options like IRAs and 401(k)s.

R oller-set curls. That little chain that keeps your glasses around your neck while you're playing bridge. Portable blood pressure monitors. Believe it or not, you may be a withered granny someday, complete with these and a closetful of the other hallmarks of old age.

Plenty of smart, shall we say "mature" Americans know how to grow old gracefully. They've planned for their future, padded their nest egg a little year after year, and learned to put off instant gratification today to save for tomorrow. Lucky them, tooling around in their new Cadillacs, dividing their time between golf games and hogging lanes on the highway in their RVs. That's the kind of retiree we'd all like to be. But if we don't start saving for it, we just might end up living in a wobbly single-wide trailer, eating Alpo for protein, and refusing to turn on the heat. With that kind of retirement on the horizon, no wonder so many people decide to keep working as long as they can stand it!

Thankfully, most companies offer a bevy of retirement plans for employees to participate in. From IRAs and 401(k)s to 403(b)s and beyond, you can start stashing pennies away now, even getting your company to match your contributions (free money!).

But retirement planning is like exercise: we all know we should do it, but just can't seem to get around to it. The truth is, beefing up on retirement financing lingo is about as exciting as watching the grass grow. "I'll care about that stuff later on," we reason. "I'm still in my twenties. I have forty more years of work ahead of me!" All the more reason to start socking it away now, say experts. Through the magic of compounding interest, the modest amount saved when you start young actually equals more than saving a large amount later in life, say in your forties.

Get comfortable with the idea of saving for your golden years while you're at your peak earning potential. Troll the new book section of your library and pick up a personal finance book or two, or check out goldandjewels.com or motleyfool.com, two excellent personal finance websites that can help you learn about investing, choose accounting software, and control your debt. Plenty of resources exist to help you master your money situation.

Next time you have a few spare minutes to kill or need a break from your current project at work, check out your company's intranet and study up on the retirement benefits your company offers. Even if you don't start contributing now, it's good to know that "IRA" doesn't just stand for a bunch of angry young Irishmen with guns.

Find out how to start participating, and play around with those nifty amortization schedules to see how many nest feathers it takes to add up to a million-dollar retirement fund. Sure, you could learn to live on less, but maybe you want to live high on the hog, going to the dinner buffet at 4:30 every day and having a bevy of eyeglass chains in a huge assortment of colors! Anyway, you'll need something to occupy all that spare time besides visiting your grandkids, and it's hard to win a spot as some young buck's sugar mama on an Alpo-size budget.

Did you know . . .

- According to a 1999 survey, 68 percent of those surveyed plan on working after they retire.
- Only half of all workers surveyed have worked the numbers to find out how much they need to save for retirement.
- Don't count on Social Security. Social Security's difficulties stem from the fact that the elderly population is increasing faster than the number of workers financing the program.
- At age fifty, 75 percent of the population has less than $5,000 in the bank for retirement.
- At age sixty-five, 23 percent of the population must still work to make ends meet.

59

Spilling the Beans

Remove that messy stain from your shirt.

> "For best results: Wash in cold water separately, hang dry,
> and iron with warm iron. For not so good results:
> Drag behind car through puddles, blow-dry on roof rack."
> —Laundry instructions on a shirt made by
> HEET (Korea)

Saving some for later, are we? Why else would a grown woman walk around the office with a bright yellow mustard stain on her new black silk shirt? Oh. You didn't see it. Unfortunately, everyone else did. They just figured you were a slob.

Now that you know it's there, what are you going to do? Sure, scrubbing it may get a good portion of the color out, but that doesn't do much for that huge wet spot on your boob! It wouldn't be such a big deal if you weren't about to go into one of the most important meetings of your career. So *now* what?

Granted, it doesn't do you much good now, but if you had kept a change of clothes in your car, this wouldn't be an issue. Not to say that you always have to keep a spare suit hanging in your rear side window at all times, but on the day of the big corporate merger, Murphy's Law says whatever *can* happen, *will*.

One thing that can be kept in your car is a long-sleeved black crewneck shirt. The color will go with anything (even brown) and the style works with any season and any type of outfit—alone, under a suit jacket, with a skirt or slacks, or even over a dress. You'll want to choose a fabric that doesn't wrinkle—unless you also feel like carrying an iron in your trunk (not a tire iron—an ironing iron).

Ditto with a pair of solid black pants. If you're not well-endowed in the chest area, the shirt may not be an issue. Drippings may fall straight from the mouth-entering food item to the upper thigh.

You may also want to keep a packet of stain removers in your purse or desk drawer. If the restroom doesn't have an air dryer (think Madonna in *Desperately Seeking Susan*), you'll have to keep a blow-dryer in your trunk or under the bathroom sink at work. If you're lucky enough to have a locker at work, it makes your task much easier.

Of course, many stains will be quick and easy to get out, and you probably won't have a major merger meeting every day. Even the "normal" days, however, can be cause for great embarrassment—even among close friends and coworkers. Spilling a huge glob of ketchup onto the crotch of your new white pants may cause a flashback to ninth grade history class as you tie your cardigan around your waist to head back to your desk. Don't worry though. According to Murphy's Law, no one was staring at the ketchup splotch because they were too busy checking out the giant chocolate stain on your butt.

60

Time Out!

Avoid acting as a referee for coworker arguments.

"Keep your friends close, but your enemies closer."
—from *The Godfather*

The tension's been building during team meetings for weeks. Two close coworkers can't seem to help shooting down each other's ideas, making catty comments to each other, and bristling whenever the other's around. Indeed, battling coworkers equal office politics of the suckiest kind, leaving you to wonder, "Why can't we all just get along?"

You, on the other hand, try to get along well with everyone and do your darnedest to remain an island of calm in the stormy seas of office politics. Complain? Never! Cattiness? Not you! (Hey, you can't help but make a snotty aside when that weird Wiccan chick from HR wears a poncho.) Those minor sins aside, what do you do when your crabby coworkers and their attitudes rain on your parade?

One way to win the office politics game is to try not to play. The next time one of the complainers comes creeping around your cubicle, subtly opt out of the conversation by saying, "Well, I need to get back to work now" and turning back to the task at hand. That usually nips nagging in the bud, and the guilty party usually gets the hint: you're too busy, or at least too much of a lady, to indulge in idle colleague bashing. If that doesn't work, simply stop the person in mid-sentence and say, "You know, unless something directly involves me personally, I don't get involved." Uttering that one slightly awkward sentence usually shuts people up.

If you just can't help but join the fray and want to do a good deed, consider orchestrating a lunch out with both complainants. Playing matchmaker and inviting them both out may get them to bury the hatchet, or at least soften the edges once they start relating to each other on a more personal level (note to self: congratulate self on master mediating skills).

Is the warring between employees who serve under you? Get ready to put your management skills to the test! If you notice employees coming to you with chronic complaints against other people in the company, try the direct approach and have a hash out session. Simply call the parties in question into your office at the same time, sit them down, and say, "I believe it's important to work out issues that come up within our team. Let's talk about the problems you two are experiencing, and ideas you have on how we can solve them and go forward with a clean slate." Trapping them in on a Friday afternoon ought to generate some solutions in a hurry.

Better yet, stick them on a long-term project together. Not to be the meanest boss in the whole wide world, but rather to get them to learn to work in tandem rather than acting like polar opposites. Just don't put one in charge of the other on the project . . . unless you really want to see some fireworks.

Another idea is to make cooperating with others part of their regular review. (You're the boss, right? You can do whatever you want!) They'll equate getting along with getting a good review and pay raise, and you'll get happy worker bees who can buzz along without trying to out-sting each other.

61

While the Cat's Away

Help maintain order when the boss travels.

Even if you haven't exactly been left in charge, there are things you'll need to take care of while the boss is away from the office for an extended period of time. Although taking messages is certainly important, there may be a few more specific ideas to help make the transition to bosslessness easier for everyone.

First and foremost, plan ahead. Ask the boss if there is anything you can do to help her plan: confirm hotel and rental car reservations, call the airport to make sure her flight is leaving on time, make sure all the yellow cabs aren't booked due to a last-minute Shriner's convention.

Don't assume that your boss has remembered everything. She could be the top CEO in New England, but that may only mean she's completely overwhelmed with too much to do in too little time. Offer to read off a checklist of items, some of which you can handle while she ties up loose ends the day before her trip. Even a "must pack" list may be helpful—especially if the trip itself is last-minute. Things like sunblock, sunglasses, a laptop, her Palm Pilot, a bathing suit, the babysitter's number, or her passport may have been forgotten.

You may also want to offer to check in on things for her while she's away. Keeping the plants in her office watered, checking with the printer to make sure the new brochures get done, or preparing all the background material for the big meeting scheduled for the day after she returns may help put her mind at ease. Don't forget about sorting her mail (priority, nonpriority, and emergency) and covering phone calls to help make her return to the office more bearable.

By helping your boss enjoy her vacation or better cope with a stressful business trip, you're sure to earn her respect and confidence. Even if the assistance doesn't lead to an immediate pay raise or promotion, it'll remind you just how good you are at your job.

62

My Aching Head

Get through a day at work with the flu.

"Natural forces within us are the true healers of disease."
—Hippocrates

You wake up in the morning feeling like death warmed over. Burning throat. You can't get warm. Aching bones where you didn't even know you had bones. Your face has a ghastly green pallor. There's only one explanation for how rotten you feel (well, you used to feel this way after a night of beer bong shots with your sorority sisters, but that's a whole different story). You have the flu!

If only you could call in sick and stay home to nurse a hot cup of tea and your health at the same time in front of a roaring fire. But you don't have any tea. You don't even have a fireplace. What you do have are deadlines, deadlines, and more deadlines to meet at work, along with FedEx guys to flirt with. Plus, it's payday and your check's waiting in your in box, aching to be misspent. If only you hadn't blown your last sick day sleeping it off the day after that big concert (it's an illness called the "day after Deftones") last month. Looks like you'll have to suffer bravely through it!

Don't panic. Today's pharmacist has enough sick-banishing pills, potions, and other stuff to cure, or at least doctor up, a host of maladies. Your local drugstore has a stockpile of pills rivaled only by Robert Downey Jr.'s medicine cabinet, along with knowledgeable pharmacists to explain the over-the-counter stuff. With an iron will and 500 mg of something in a capsule pumping through your system, you'll be able to power through your day long enough to make it home and collapse on the couch.

What if you're one of the brave souls who opts for going the natural route without drugs? Try one of these natural remedies to help beat the flu:

* At the onset of symptoms, take Echinacea three times a day to boost your immune system. Don't forget to take good old vitamin C supplements, too.
* A teaspoon of vitamin C–packed grated horseradish in boiling water (yummy!) chases away winter chills. Eat plenty of garlic to build up your resistance (as well as the resistance of your significant other when he catches a whiff of you) . . .
* Try ginger tea or ginger ale to alleviate nausea. Old ginger or "mother ginger" found at Chinese or herb markets is particularly potent.
* Stay hydrated.
* For congestion relief, try steeping fresh parsley in boiling water for two minutes. Better yet, eat something spicy to get that sinus plumbing opened up.

Once you're at work, slather on a hand sanitizer gel and encourage coworkers to do the same. It may be too little too late for you, but consider the comfort of currently healthy coworkers. Not only do you not want to reinfect yourself, but any coworkers who catch the bug a few days after you will resent you for turning your cubicle into a cootie hatchery.

63

Been There, Done That

Create a killer résumé.

> *"Talent does what it can; genius does what it must."*
> **—Edward George Bulwer-Lytton**

So you're looking for a new job, eh? Don't expect that your old résumé from 1994 will still cut it. At the time, your biggest achievement was stacking two scoops of double chocolate chunk without it falling off the cone. It's time to update your résumé and show your soon-to-be boss what you've accomplished since Meadowgold Creamery signed your checks.

The Format

When it comes to the paper on which you'll print your résumé, opt for a medium to heavy bond in off-white. Grays or creams are appropriate as well, but stay away from brights or excessively ornate letterhead. Always use black ink. Whenever possible, purchase matching full-size (9" by 12") envelopes to avoid folding your résumé.

Your résumé's layout should follow the KISS rule of thumb: Keep It Simple, Stupid.

Center your name, address, phone number, and E-mail address at the top, followed by your work experience (chronologically from most recent to oldest). Next, list your education, relevant skills, and the old "References Available Upon Request" line.

Some experts believe that an objective (e.g., "Seeking a sales position that allows me to use my management skills at a Fortune 500 company.") should be listed above your work experience, while others argue that it can imply you're inflexible.

Things to Avoid

* Using an E-mail address that appears unprofessional, such as HotMama@yahoo.com. Instead, sign up for a free E-mail service using your name in the address.
* Cutting old jobs. Beginner's jobs, such as fast-food work, show you've progressed and that you worked hard—even at a young age. For example, waitressing jobs can show organization, people skills, customer service, and multitasking.
* Listing irrelevant skills (such as cutting hair when you're applying for a marketing job). Instead, include things like typing, reading comprehension, and second (or third) languages.
* Sharing personal information such as age, graduation date, marital status, and number of children.
* Typos.
* Sending long résumés. Résumés should be one to two pages. Any longer and you may overload the interviewer.

Things to Include

* Achievements, such as increasing revenue for a past company.
* Accomplishments and promotions, such as being named "Employee of the Month" or moving up the corporate ladder.
* Items that show you're a team player.

* Position/title, company, and dates at job.
* Responsibilities you had at each job.
* Specific skills you have to offer the new job.
* A cover letter. This should be addressed to the appropriate person by (last) name and include the position for which you are applying. Don't assume it's the only opening the company has, or you could learn too late that you're being interviewed for the janitorial gig.

After a week, call to check on the status of your application and ask about any additional information, such as references, that may help you get your foot in the door. Don't be afraid to apply for more than one job at a time. The worst that will happen is a tug-of-war over you between two companies. Either way, you win.

64

Desktop Doldrums

Redecorate your office or cubicle for a fresh outlook.

"What I wanted to be when I grew up was—in charge."
—Wilma Vaught

It's the little things that can influence your day: ever notice how you feel recharged and energized after cleaning your office and putting a few pictures around? Taking a few minutes to tidy up and decorate your office space can make a crucial difference in your attitude at work.

Assuming you have your own space or at least your own desktop, you can go hog wild while carefully staying within that space. If you're lucky enough to have your own cubicle or office, pick a color or design theme to go from. Flip through interior design magazines for more ideas, and don't be afraid to choose a "nonoffice" look. Then choose wall hangings, floor coverings, and other accessories that work for you.

Before buying that $600 area rug, be sure decorating your office or cube is OK with the powers that be. Companies usually don't care, as long as the funds you use to decorate are your own and you leave the "Beefcake Boys of Summer" calendar at home. Consider whether or not clients will visit your workspace, which will help decide whether you want to present yourself as a seasoned professional to the world (lots of leather accessories and high-quality picture frames), or go for the zany individualist look (rubber chicken, your kid's finger paintings, Mardi Gras beads, etc.).

Want maximum panache with minimal effort? Try these ideas:

Posters. Many hobby stores have preframed posters at great prices.

Calendars. Whether inspirational, humorous, or somewhere in between, choose wall and desk calendars that speak to you. Better yet, choose a few—then there will be no excuse for asking, "What day is this, again?" when you go to write a check on the way home.

Rugs. Any fun little area rug will cozy up the place. Pick something low shedding and low maintenance, or risk inciting the wrath of the night janitor.

Fresh flowers. Truly temporary, but very classy. Daisies, lilacs from the neighbor's bush, and cheapie carnations offer as much aromatherapy and ambiance as expensive roses.

Feng shui for the office. In the ancient ways of feng shui, success is all about placement. Not getting that big promotion you hoped for? Maybe your desk is in the wrong bagua! Peruse sites like fengshuipalace.com for details on which elements enhance your career.

Lamps. From lava to Tiffany to beaded, a simple lamp or two can emit a radiant glow. Fluorescent lights bugging you? Switch to lamps so you can control your own lighting.

Illuminating Facts About the Lava Lamp

According to the oozinggoo.com website, the lava lamp was originally invented by Englishman Craven Walker. According to the patent, the lava consists of a solidified globule of mineral oil with a light paraffin, carbon tetrachloride, a dye, and paraffin wax.

65

Six Degrees of Separation

Get the most out of a networking meeting.

"The difference between 'involvement' and 'commitment' is like an eggs-and-ham breakfast: the chicken was 'involved'—the pig was 'committed.'"
—Unknown

Ever since the Le Petite Chalet incident, you don't need to be told to check for toilet paper hanging off your heel. Or your dress being tucked in your panty hose. (It was a really, *really* bad night.)

If this sort of thing has ever happened to you and you feel like a networking nincompoop, don't be embarrassed. Networking with finesse is not necessarily something we're taught in business school or during our two-week training period. Still, we *have* been told that networking is one of our greatest ways to generate business and visibility. Use the following tips to help you not only generate leads, but make yourself memorable to the people you've met at a networking meeting.

1. **Build partnerships.** Ask the event's host or the person who invited you to introduce you to another small business owner with whom you may be able to build a partnership. If you're a copywriter, for example, ask to be introduced to a printer. His existing (and future) clients may need a copywriter for brochures, catalogs, and advertis-

ing inserts. In return, offer to hand out his business card and rate sheets as referrals to *your* clients.

2. **Talk about your *needs*, not your business.** Whenever possible, give a very brief synopsis of your business (say, one to three sentences, depending on how complicated your industry is), then focus more on sharing what leads you're seeking.

For example, instead of saying, "I'm a Realtor" and then talking about how many houses you've sold, focus more on the fact that you're always looking to help low-income women who are still renting or couples that are ready to move into a bigger house to start a family. By specifying your needs, you'll help your listener visualize a "target market" that may lead him or her to offer a name immediately—or a referral later.

3. **Do your follow-ups immediately.** Unless you own a very specialized business, chances are you're not the only rep in your industry at the event. If you're a Web designer and John Smith casually mentions that he knows a company that is toying with the idea of building a website, at the very least get John's phone number. Call John the next business day and offer to send information to the company he mentioned. If you wait too long, one of three things may happen: (1) the company may find someone else; (2) John may forget who you are and/or what company he was referring to; or (3) the *other* Web designer that was at the mixer might call John first.

You may even want to throw in a referral for John if you end up closing the deal with the company he recommended. The incentive may be enough for him to put in a good word with the company.

4. **Listen more than you talk.** Have you ever walked away from a luncheon in which you monopolized the conversation, only to think, "Wow. That guy is great!" In reality, you're responding to that person's ability to make you feel important. Listening is not only a great way to impress the talker, but also to allow you to hear information (read: hot leads!) that you might otherwise not have heard. Generally, the

more comfortable someone feels with you, the more he or she will be willing to share personally and professionally.

5. **Don't be a stranger.** Friendly faces are always a sight for sore eyes at business functions. By turning casual acquaintances into friendships, you're sure to start getting more referrals. In addition, each opportunity allows you to reiterate your business needs and any new products or services you're now offering.

6. **Reciprocate the invitation.** Gathering business cards serves more of a purpose than just referrals. The next time you hold an open house (or possibly even your *own* mixer), you have a new list of invitees.

7. **Take notes.** Use the space on the back of the business cards you gather to write down tidbits of information to jog your memory later. A note like "Cathy's daughter starts at Harvard in September" will give you a personal touch when you contact Cathy in the future. "Hi, Cathy. This is Jessica from XYZ Company. We met at that Chamber mixer two months ago. So how's your daughter's course load at Harvard?" Cathy will most likely be shocked, touched, and impressed by your attention to detail—a quality that most people in the business community admire.

66

The Big Picture

Put career goals on a twelve-month calendar.

> *"First say to yourself what you would be;*
> *and then do what you have to do."*
> **—Epictetus**

Most of us need no convincing that a to-do list is a great idea. It seems like the mere act of writing down the things you need to do today can infinitely increase the possibility that stuff will actually *get done* (what a concept!).

It's pinning down those long-term to-dos that can be a bit squirrelly. Writing down "enter M.B.A. classes nine months from now, after financial aid application is approved" is dandy, but how does that translate into an action item you can tackle today? What's more, how does a girl keep track of long-term dreams and goals without cluttering up today's list of important tasks?

Get a twelve-month wall calendar or other long-term planner and turn those vague, career-related "I oughta" notions (take a class, rally for a promotion, open your own company, shop for a power suit . . . you name it) into grand accomplishments.

The process is easy. Where do you want to be one year from now in your career? Simply take that ultimate goal and break it into smaller, achievable steps, to be spread out over the upcoming year. Then pencil those benchmarks onto a master calendar. For example, if your goal is to become head of your department in one year, you may need to (1) take a management seminar in the next month, (2) ask for more responsibility in your current position within the next three months, and (3) obtain a job description of the job you want and compare your qualifications within six months, etc.

Sounds easy, doesn't it? Charting goals is easy—sticking to them all and seeing your goal through to completion is where it gets challenging.

If you're a visual person, a twelve-month wipe-off calendar is the best way to go. Make sure to choose one with days large enough to allow you plot out plenty of details to your to-do items. Maybe tape a big manila envelope to the back of the calendar or in the corner to keep related flyers, notes, and class registration handy, to help you take immediate action on the stuff on your calendar. Depending on your ultimate goal, you may want to keep your long-term calendar in an inconspicuous place—especially if you have a controversial goal like ousting your boss to steal her job, or to earn enough credibility and experience to get a better job elsewhere.

Do you prefer a filing system? Consider getting a tickler file, one of those accordion-like expanding files. Get one that arranges filing slots by month (weekly is even better). File upcoming memos, class registrations, or other information in your tickler file, and refer to it regularly to see what's on tap for you.

To reinforce the goals you've set on your calendar, consider using an E-mail reminder service. Websites like memotome.com, rememberit.com, pcreminder.com, and neverforget.com allow you to E-mail a personal reminder to yourself weeks, even months away. Friendly reminders from cyberspace will help you stay on task as you pursue your Next Big Thing.

And when will that Next Big Thing come to fruition, exactly? That's easy: just check on your long-term calendar!

67

Brainpower!

Stimulate your brain with puzzles,
tests, and word problems.

> *"If you think your boss is stupid, remember:
> you wouldn't have a job if he was smarter."*
> —**Albert Grant**

Just because you sometimes have to do mind-numbing tasks doesn't mean you can't stimulate your brain in other ways. If you've spent the entire morning addressing holiday cards for the company's 1,268 clients, your mind may be as cramped as your writing hand.

To get a quick fix of synaptic energy, keep your desk drawer stocked full of crossword puzzle books, brainteasers, or IQ tests to do on your break or lunch hour.

Depending on your level of interest (have you been doing crosswords for years?) and just how far you've been thrust into the throes of a boredom-related coma, you'll need to choose your stash wisely. The *New York Times* is world-renowned for its steep puzzlers, while your local paper's daily crossword may allow for a sense of completion.

Most Sunday papers also have at least one Word Jumble puzzle where the letters need to be unscrambled to form common (or not-so-common) words. There are also bridge games, comics, and horoscopes to keep your mind off your work. The choice is yours. *Games* magazine is also jam-packed full of every kind of puzzle you can imagine. From word, picture, and number games to Mensa-type tests and logic brainteasers, each issue is probably enough to keep you busy for the month. Just be prepared to be bald from all the hair you'll be pulling out in frustration.

There are plenty of websites that offer games, brainteasers, and crossword puzzles, too. Problem is, if you've been doing work on your computer all day, then staring at the screen through your entire lunch hour may not exactly seem like a break. Luckily, most sites will let you print out the games so you could have a new crossword every day for the rest of your career if you wanted.

If you're not into crossword puzzles, IQ tests are as fun as they are varied. The Web is full of fun sites to see how you measure up.

If you'd rather have a more colorful challenge, pick up that old eighties favorite, the Rubik's Cube, at Spencer Gifts or your nearest novelty shop. While you're there, you may even run across another favorite: Mad Libs. Get a few coworkers together at lunch and bust a gut while you stretch your word power with a "Mad Libs for the Verbose." You'll learn a few new words and show off your own grammatical prowess.

Guess those IQ scores were right on the money!

Online Crosswords

Looking for some online crosswords? Check out these brainteasers:

crossword-puzzles.com.uk
phillynews.com/crossword
dictionary.com/fun/crossword
nytimes.com/diversions
bestcrosswords.com
nanana.com/crosswordpuzzles.htm

Need help with some of the toughies? Check out oneacross.com for some help with the impossible clues for crossword puzzles or anagrams.

68

Effective E-Mailing

Squelch E-mail time squandering.

> *"The Internet is so big, so powerful and pointless that for some people it is a complete substitute for life."*
> **—Andrew Brown**

Isn't it amazing the way the Internet and E-mail allow instant communication with anyone, almost anywhere in the world? Information can be exchanged between people in different countries, making important business data (or your aunt's muffin recipe) instantly accessible. What's more, this technology is available on practically every home and business desktop in America.

Between checking your daily E-horoscope, checking with your friends about weekend plans, and monitoring your recent eBay bid, a girl can hardly get work in edgewise. But whether it's wielded to monitor crucial department communiqués or just to flirt with Hal from accounting, some E-mail etiquette guidelines are in order.

Anyone who's ever used E-mail knows it's also easy to abuse. Heck, some would even call it addictive, and the urge to reach out and E-mail someone can have you checking your E-mail every four minutes. That's harmless enough—unless you're compelled to neglect the burgeoning mountain of work on your desk because your E-mail use is sucking up all your time. Check it at preset times, not every time you think about it. That alone will save you the few minutes it takes to log on and peer into your virtual mailbox. Also, inquire about your company's E-mail policies. If it has a "Big Brother" policy in place where it can monitor use, you may be cut off from E-mail altogether if you're spending too much time on it.

Be sure to answer short E-mail requests when you open them, rather than saving them for later. There's no sense saving a message and retrieving it when it would take thirty seconds or less to simply send an answer. And make a habit of adding addresses to your E-mail book, rather than writing them down. This saves time and builds a handy little resource for you. The next time the lights above your cubicle go out, rather than scouring the company directory for that guy you E-mail occasionally in maintenance, you'll scroll through and dash a request off to Terry@maintenance.xyz.com.

Some rules for sending are in order as well. Most business professionals recommend eschewing emoticons. Keep smiley faces, LOLs, and other cute icons to a minimum. Emoticons in business communications are taboo, and there's a chance the stuffy CEO you're communicating with may not know the meaning you're trying to convey, anyway.

Give recipients the abridged version of your message by keeping messages to the point. In E-language, lengthy messages are akin to endlessly scrolling text . . . get to the point. Spare the chatty prose for a handwritten letter.

Beware the add-ons, too. Don't forward attachments without asking the recipient first, lest you cause his or her computer to freeze and so incur wrath. The recipient may not have the software capability to download a file successfully, and won't appreciate the computer freakout a bad attachment may cause. What's more, you may unwittingly pass a virus attached to the file, since not all virus scanning software works 100 percent of the time.

Finally, use extra caution when submitting confidential information, being sure to double-check the recipient name. If possible, disable your E-mail software's autofill function, so it won't automatically fill in a name after the first three characters. This is crucial if your boss, best friend, and mom all have similar initials or E-mail addresses. You don't want to accidentally send a scathing note to your ex-boyfriend at mark.w@xyz.com and find out a second too late you just sent it to "mark.e@xyz.com."

69

The Sweet Smell of Success

Perk, soothe, and de-stress with aromatherapy.

"Accept that some days you're the pigeon, and some days you're the statue."
—Scott Adams

You've seen the videos on MTV: the gorgeous woman is up to her neck in a hot bubble bath surrounded by glowing candles that seem to illuminate her face as she lets the troubles of her day melt away.

In reality, you'd have to scrub the tub for an hour just to get the cat footprints and soap scum off the sides, and you wouldn't even need a plug seeing as the drain is jammed full of hair.

Still, there are ways to enjoy the scent of candles without breaking any fire codes at the office, namely, aromatherapy. Even if you're not into New Age practices, you have to admit that scent is a powerful tool to change your state. Just think how some of your favorite smells from childhood—chocolate chip cookies, freshly cut grass, lemonade—can take you back to fifth grade. Smells are powerful enough to help you cross over from the hectic business world of chaos to the more serene experience that most of us crave.

In addition to the brain chemistry that kicks in from aromatherapy (using scent to change your physical, mental, and emotional state), frequent use of the same smell may eventually create a Pavlovian response, signaling your body to relax whenever you dab on the scented body oil or inhale the scent of your potpourri satchel.

There are things to consider, however. First of all, your company may have a policy against spraying aerosol on the premises. Even if it doesn't, your nearest coworker may complain about the scent. "I'm allergic to everything cherry. Would you mind?"

There's also a chance that someone will accuse you of being a witch, a religious freak, or worse—a New Ager! Can you imagine the look on the CEO's face when he learns that his head negotiator is *meditating* before the big acquisition meeting? What next—you'll be doing yoga and eating vegetarian food?!

If you have your own office with a door that locks, most of these problems can be avoided. In fact, no one has to know you're creating a peaceful day for yourself with the help of lovely scents. As long as you don't have any open flames, you should be OK.

You'll need to learn a few basics in aromatherapy before you get started. The last thing you want to do is work against your own energy. If you need to mellow out at the end of the day, you may want to stay away from an energizing scent like peppermint. Likewise, if you're trying to rev yourself up to be a spitfire before the meeting with the attorneys, chamomile might settle you down a bit too much. Then again, if you're going to be swimming with the sharks, it's better to smell like chamomile than chum. Do they even *make* that scent?

Did you know . . .

- A study found that office workers complete 13.5 percent more paperwork and supermarket shoppers buy 38.2 percent more food if Muzak is playing in the background.
- Forty percent of all office memos are unnecessary. The main problems of memos are that they are too long, too self-serving, and routed to too many people.

70

"Stalling" for Time

Stake out the handicapped stall and take a breather
to clear the day from your head.

*"I believe every human has a finite number of heartbeats. I don't
intend to waste any of mine running around doing exercises."*
—**Neil Armstrong**

Cubicle dwellers don't know how good they've got it. Sure, you're a rat in a maze. But, you have your own little private space to surreptitiously stretch out, do some deep breathing, and touch up your lipstick without being pestered. Other working girls who deal with the public, from teachers to cashiers to hash-slingers, are "on" all the time. Ask any elementary school teacher, and she'll tell you she can't even go to the can without being stopped ten times on the way. In fact, it seems the bathroom is the last bastion of privacy there is these days in workplaces with glass office doors and office sharing.

Which brings up an interesting point. If you need a breather but it's not break time (as if anyone takes those these days!) flee to the solitude of the stall. Hey, don't laugh! The ladies' room may be lowly, but at least it's quiet (usually), you can get a minute alone, and there's no phone, client, or colleague demanding your attention. We may be living in an age where it's usual for coworkers to interrupt you mid–phone call, or barge into any office, but the bathroom is still private.

Sounds twisted, but if you need a breather, head for the head. Choose the handicapped stall since it's roomier. Just make sure you're not hogging it when someone with a wheelchair or walker needs it.

Finally alone? Time to really let go! Do some side stretches, toe touching, and deep breathing. Indulge yourself in a little three-minute yoga routine that will have you refreshed in a jiffy without making coworkers wonder where you've been.

Try these maximum moves. Do head rolls from side to side, to stretch out those tired neck muscles. Next, press your chin to your chest and take a few deep breaths. Inhale and raise your shoulders up to your ears as high as they'll go. Repeat until you're feeling rubbery.

Next, bend at the waist and touch your toes. Power up this stretch by bending one leg at a time once your toes are touched. Even if yoga's not your thing, it's your three minutes. The world inside the stall is your oyster! Clear your mind by trying some creative visualization: picture a blue sky, fluffy clouds, your puppy dog—anything you find relaxing. Feel free to kick off your shoes and rub your feet.

Feeling extra limber? Pretend the grip bar is a ballet bar and kick your heel around it for a super ballerina-style stretch. With one leg up on the bar, bend your other leg (called a plié in dance) for added oomph. Careful though: one wrong move and your suede pump will go "plop" in the toilet. Try explaining that one to the gang once you get back to your desk.

Finish your solitary stall time up with a quickie scalp massage, guaranteed to make your brain happy. Massage your scalp vigorously with the pads of your fingers, working your way from the front to the nape of your neck. Aaahhh!

71

Miss Personality

Take a break and complete an online personality test
to match up with your dream job.

> *"A good rule of thumb is if you've made it to thirty-five
> and your job still requires you to wear a name tag,
> you've made a serious vocational error."*
> **—Dennis Miller**

D o you ever wonder what the statistics are regarding people who really love their jobs? Sure, there are probably tons who say they're living their dream life, but chances are they are either sitting in front of their boss at the time, or are surfers.

In reality, your job is probably just that: a job. For some women it's a career choice, but for most it's something you took to pay the bills, get out of the house, or get experience.

But what's a girl to do—just up and quit and hope that a dream job falls in her lap? Hardly. Changing to a better-suited job isn't a matter of just picking up the classifieds. First you have to know what you're looking for.

There are lots of personality tests that you can take online to help you figure out what you want to be "when you grow up." Even if you're only twenty-five, there's no rule that says you have to change jobs seventeen times to figure out what makes you happy. Why can't you learn early and be fortunate enough to find something you love?

Start by thinking back to what you loved to do as a child. Were you always playing dress-up? Maybe you'd like to be a fashion designer or actress. Did you enjoy baking cookies? Perhaps you'd enjoy being a chef or opening your own restaurant. Do you remember drawing? Singing? Making forts? Playing doctor? (Never mind that last one. That had nothing to do with wanting to go into medicine, did it?)

If you can't find a personality test, you may be able to solicit some advice from friends, family, and coworkers. Try asking them a few questions that might help you see your attributes more clearly:

* What do you think I'm really good at? E.g., negotiating, mediating, singing, working with clients, writing, editing, cooking.
* In what occupation do you think I'd be most happy?
* What part of my job do you think I do best and why?
* What part of my job do I need work on?
* What do you remember me saying I enjoyed doing as a child?

Whatever approach you choose, don't feel any pressure to follow through on all (or any!) of the career results that pop up. Remember, most women are naturally caring, loving, multitasking givers—that doesn't mean you have to become the next Mother Teresa. They don't have hair dryers, sushi, or Chanel in India, and although your boss is forgiving, he doesn't miss anything. (But the retirement plan can't be beat.)

Speaking of personality tests . . .

Check out these online personality tests to get a better idea of what careers are best suited for you:
- Type Focus evaluation at http://typefocus.com
- Advisor Team's personality test at advisorteam.com

- A career competency questionnaire at http://content.monster.com/tools/personality/links
- Soul Inspiration's self-evaluation at soulinspiration.com/self-assessment.htm
- For a search directory for a variety of tests check out allthetests.com

Or these books:
- *Ace the Corporate Personality Test* by Edward Hoffman
- *The Essential Enneagram: The Definitive Personality Test and Self-Discovery Guide* by David N. Daniels

72

Working the Graveyard Shift Gracefully

Consistency is the key in adjusting to
an off-kilter work schedule.

"The beginning of health is sleep."
—Irish proverb

Your friends who complain about having to work late ("I had to work till 6:30 Friday night. Ugh!") don't know how good they've got it. You're on the night shift, which usually means all your previously held notions of "off time" and peak working hours get thrown out the window as you struggle to adjust to a work schedule that only a zombie could love.

More than ever, businesses are expanding their reach by expanding their operating hours. Many companies stay open twenty-four hours a day. If you're a graveyard or swing shift worker, you may find that adjusting to an off-kilter schedule is no small task. Even with catching up on sleep, you may find yourself dragging around on your off hours. Why's it so tough to stay awake? Because your body's natural rhythms, or circadian clock, are tied to the world's natural dark and light patterns of sunlight, so it's ingrained in you to sleep when it's dark and be awake when it's light.

You can't fool Mother Nature, but you can try a few things to beat the graveyard shift blues. In fact, there's plenty you can do to get the best shut-eye possible. On the way home from work, wear wraparound sunglasses to keep those UV rays from signaling your brain with a message of "good morning, wake up!"

Once home, make sleep a serious priority: get blackout shades for your bedroom to keep the light from disturbing you. Those Hollywood-looking dark eye masks work well, if you prefer not to invest in new bedroom shades. Splurge on a supercomfy pillow and quality sheets, if you haven't done so. Ask friends or roommates to banish dishwashing, TV, or other distracting noise during your sleep time. Don't forget to turn the ringer off before you crash—even important calls can be returned once you're awake, but your health depends on getting quality, uninterrupted sleep.

Tough as it may seem, maintaining a consistent sleep schedule is a big part of adjusting to the graveyard shift. As tempting as it is to think you're off during the day and can therefore run errands, your health and sanity depend on quality sleep. Sleeping during the day all week and then trying to stay up through the day until midnight on weekends will only wreak havoc with your energy level and mood. Rather than reverting to a day worker's hours and snoozing at night, try using your job as the perfect excuse to be a bad influence: make your friends stay up all night long and crash at 7 A.M., just like you do!

When you finally do get off work, make the most of sleep time by being aware of inhibiting stuff that disrupts sleep patterns. Some antidepressants are rumored to interfere with sleep. Ask your doctor about this, or you'll wind up depressed *and* tired. Know yourself and the effects of alcohol and caffeine on your body. Does an afternoon soda pop leave you jittery all evening? Then stay away from the "false high" and snooze-inhibiting soda mid–graveyard shift. Conversely, don't opt for wine with dinner, then show up at 10:00 P.M. for your shift and expect to be bushy tailed.

Finally, try the old-fashioned sleep remedies of a glass of warm milk or chamomile tea if you have trouble getting to sleep. Watch out for sleeping pills: if there's a nonmedicinal way to nod off, choose it before popping a potentially addictive pill.

Good Night

Check out sleepfoundation.org, sleepnet.com, and powersleep.org for more information on the importance of sleep.

73

Loose Lips Sink Ships

Beat the office gossip at her own game.

"They say women talk too much. If you have worked in Congress you know that the filibuster was invented by men."
—Clare Boothe Luce

What's faster than a speeding bullet or a locomotive? No, not Superman: *office gossip.*

Don't believe it? Here's a little test. Spread a rumor about yourself (preferably a good one) to the office gossip and see how fast it takes to get back to you. How about something juicy but not so awful that it'll get you fired. It will also have to be something that you can prove isn't true. How about that your father is famous? (You'll have to be the illegitimate daughter so they can't check it out on the Internet.) Yes, that'll be fun. Now to choose the right pop . . .

Bill Gates? Could be a tough sell, depending on your age. Also, if your boss finds out, you can either kiss that promotion good-bye ("She certainly doesn't need the money.") or get it only because your boss is kissing up ("The boss gave her a raise in hopes he'd get to meet her dad.").

Bill Clinton? Believable considering his past actions, but highly doubtful.

Bill Cosby? Depends what you look like. Ditto with Billy D. Williams.

Best bet? Bill Bixby. (You know, the guy who played the tame side of the Incredible Hulk.)

The point is, pick someone who everyone will know, but who won't be too high profile. You'll be surprised how fast Olive, the office gossip, can lattice the company grapevine. Maybe she'll learn her lesson once you embarrass her a bit with some harmless fun. "So listen, Olive. I'm telling you this in the strictest confidence. Please don't tell anyone . . ."

Before you know it, you'll be asked if your dad ever turned green when he was yelling at you. You can just laugh and say, "Yes. He turned *olive* green in fact" and nod in the direction of Olive's office. Most of the staff will be probably be familiar with her antics and understand exactly what you're talking about.

Sure, you can always approach Olive head-on, but that may not embarrass her enough to get her to change her ways. Your best bet may be to wait until someone else is in the room with you, asking about your dad, and say, "Where did you ever get that crazy idea?" When the person explains that Olive told him, there's bound to be an awkward moment as Olive scrambles to defend herself.

Of course, you could also teach Olive a lesson by beating her at her own game of spreading private news like wildfire in a bamboo forest. Why not start a rumor that she's a spy for the boss? That ought to keep everyone from telling her anything personal, and it will be a tough one to shake off. After all, what's the first thing a spy does? Deny everything. And the second thing? Start making plea bargains. "If you tell everyone the truth—that I'm not a spy for the boss—I'll stop gossiping. I swear!"

If all else fails, you'll just have to check under the stalls when you're in the ladies room telling your coworker what happened on Saturday night. Your attempts at silencing Olive may have left her shaken—but not stirred.

74

Kiss Me Kate

Steer clear of the office dating pool.

"Romance should never begin with sentiment.
It should begin with science and end with a settlement."
—Oscar Wilde

It's been said that you should never dip your pen in company ink. Yet millions of people choose to ignore that sage advice. How many couples have you met who say, "Oh, we met at work"? Still, for every successful lunch-hour liaison, heaven only knows how many jobs have been lost to on-the-job lust. Don't let yours be one of them!

In order to fend off unwanted attention from coworkers, you need some effective reject strategies to squelch such goings-on.

We'll call the first workplace flirt encounter the Reject Rebuff maneuver. That's where you expertly nip all advances in the bud without coming across as cold and forever being labeled as the snotty chick from HR. Invariably, it's not the hardbody warehouse guy who decides to chat you up and asks you along for a flirty lunchtime fast-food run. Rather, it's when you just started a new job and some guy consistently skulks around your office, chitchatting about his personal life and working up the nerve to ask you out: "You're probably going out with your boyfriend this weekend, huh? You do have a boyfriend, right?"

Here's your golden opportunity to nip it in the bud in two seconds flat, whether you have a man or not. "Yes, I have a boyfriend," you say with a smile, then drop it. Ninety percent of guys will never flirt again in an effort to spare their ego. It's those stubborn 10 percent whose credo is "persistence (a.k.a. wearing you down in an attempt for a pity date) will pay off" that you have to worry about. Try the straightforward approach: with a gentle tone, simply say, "I'm very flattered, but I don't believe in dating coworkers."

Let's say your problem is the annoying guy who just can't help making unwanted comments about anything and everything, from your hemline to your hairstyle. Do these sound familiar?

"Look who just walked in late. What's the matter, did you have a late night last night?"

"Geez, you think your shirt/skirt is tight/short enough? How am I supposed to get any work done?"

"Man, I'm so glad it's Friday. What are you doing this weekend? I'm hitting all the singles bars and I'm gonna score, score, score!"

Your reply? Stony silence! Hasn't this fool ever heard of sexual harassment? Harmless comments that border on banal are best avoided, but if it ever reaches the point where you're uncomfortable, speak up—to your supervisor, whose job it is to intercede. She'll most likely tell him he's being a pig and threaten to take action, which gets you off the hook.

Unless it's the hardbody from the warehouse department whose suggestive comments get you in a tizzy. In that case, we don't need to tell you that the ball's in your court.

75

Gag Me with a Spoon

Let it go when competing with the "I love my job"
motivational poster child.

*"If you step on people in this life you're going to
come back as a cockroach."*
—**Willie Davis**

"Yes, sir."

"Right away, sir."

"I'd be happy to, sir."

Ever since Kiss-Butt Kathleen came on board you (and half your
office) have had the sudden urge to yell, "Cut the crap, Kathleen!"
Unfortunately (or fortunately for your job security), you instead opt
for rolling your eyes and reverting to your favorite eighties phrase,
"Gag me with a spoon."

Kathleen's antics have gone far beyond the usual intern wanna-be
butt-kissing or the "I'm up for a promotion next week" temporary
sucking up. Kathleen's lips are on permanent pucker and the worst
part is, your boss probably doesn't even realize how annoyingly fake
her responses are.

It's important to remember that in some cases, bosses are high up
the chain of command because they've earned it for their intelligence,
wisdom, and ability to see through cheesy, corporate-ladder-climbing
facades. There are still others who are at the top because they weren't

afraid to take advantage of others. Either way, don't underestimate your boss's levels of perception.

As long as you don't see a promotion in Kathleen's immediate future, try to let it go. You know what they say about finding fault in those we envy. Are you sure you're not just jealous because she gets all of the boss's attention (not to mention dry cleaning)? Sure, you could always step up to the plate and take a swing at a little butt-kissing yourself, but it's always better to work your way to the top because you deserve it. Why not just put in some extra hours or work especially hard on your next project in order to impress the boss with your creative ideas instead of your ability to make homemade chocolate chip cookies without burning them (or eating all the dough)?

Whatever your position, there's a way to do it more effectively, efficiently—and impressively! Go above and beyond your next assignment to legitimately impress your boss. Need to type a memo? Make your own suggestions on how he might be able to spice it up. Asked to do research on your competition? Take the extra time to research a few of the other companies your boss might not even know about.

Either way, give your boss some assistance—and credit. He might know more about Kathleen's tactics than you think. It's your job to make sure he knows about yours.

Did you know . . .

For every dollar earned by white men in 1998, white women earned seventy-eight cents, African-American women earned sixty-seven cents, and Hispanic women earned fifty-six cents. (**Source:** U.S. Department of Labor, Bureau of Labor Statistics, *Highlights of Women's Earnings in 1998*)

76

ftudent Driver

Give back by working with interns.

> *"Your most precious possession is not your financial assets.*
> *Your most precious possession is the people you have*
> *working there, and what they carry around in their heads,*
> *and their ability to work together."*
> **—Robert Reich**

The concept of using interns in the workplace makes a heck of a lot of sense. The interns get valuable real-life work experience and a peek at a potential long-term career, plus college credit for their trouble. The business in turn gets fresh-faced newbies who are not yet jaded, their budding spirits blissfully uncrushed by crabby coworkers and tedious office politics. Interns are often willing to go above and beyond to help in hopes of scoring a permanent position with a company after graduation.

What's more, working with interns is your chance to give back and help a budding member of your chosen profession, look like a hero, and score some free (or dirt cheap) labor. Interns rarely grouse when it comes time to tackle necessary yet mundane office tasks like filing outdated service claims and making endless copies, whereas other employees may cop an attitude: like when the file clerk says, "Copy stuff?! Ugh! What do you take me for, a file clerk?"

Most interns are very motivated to make an impression and gain experience. If you're serving as the intern's point person, try to find his or her strong points. Maybe she doesn't get the hang of answering phones, but happens to be a computer whiz who'll get your backup tapes organized and updated in a jiff. Or maybe his customer service skills are lacking, but he has a winning way with coordinating internal distributors. Discovering interns' interests and strengths is a win-win situation. They'll shine at a job well done and build confidence, while you'll get through a Monday without fixing stuff they've messed up.

Just think: train them right and you just may have an underling for life. Plenty of people graduate from internship to full-fledged full-time employee, and you'll get the credit for finding an undiscovered scholastic gem who may rise to the rank of CEO someday. That's preferable to the opposite result of choosing the one intern who accidentally sets off the alarm and locks himself out of the building a record number of times. If so, think of it this way: how long can one semester last?

👓 Looking for a Few Good Interns?

To find interns, contact your local community college. Even small schools have programs in place to match talented undergrads with corporations in need of help. Typically, the only requirements for the business are a willingness to provide regular reports and "grade" the intern at the end of the semester, since his or her work earns college credit.

77

The Screener

Understand the job of the receptionist.

There's a reason they're referred to as "gatekeepers."

The word *receptionist* literally translates from the Latin for "one who guards the reception area like a supermodel at a buffet table." Unlike her coworkers, the receptionist's job is to filter the office from the distractions of the outside world—namely, solicitors, bill collectors, and annoying phone calls.

Sure, some gatekeepers take this responsibility above and beyond, deeming themselves capable of determining who should and should not receive even *wanted* visitors and phone calls. But the unlawful screens are generally not cause for concern for those who treat the front desk queen with respect.

Being a receptionist may actually be one of the most difficult positions in the company, mainly due to the need for multitasking. In what other job do you need to file, type, edit, greet, call, answer calls, plan, copy, fax, and E-mail for someone else's needs—all in one day. Add to the scenario the fact that she needs to keep a smile on her face even when an irate customer comes through the front door, screaming at the top of his lungs about something she didn't even do.

Although you may already be aware of the importance of a secretary's (a.k.a. receptionist, personal assistant, administrative assistant, office manager) role at the company, your coworkers may not. Feel free to enlighten them when you overhear them gossiping about your friend at the front desk. "Boy, I'm surprised to hear you say anything negative about Marcia. She's the best receptionist this company has ever had. Maybe if you changed jobs with her for a day you'd understand just how difficult her position is."

This isn't to say that your company's "Marcia" is always an angel. Anyone who works under such stressful conditions (and such a demanding boss!) is bound to need to vent sometimes. Although you may want to offer to be a sounding board, be careful about what you are and are not willing to hear. (If you *are* the receptionist, read: Be careful who you bitch to!) Learning that the boss has asked her to revise the "massive layoff memo" may keep you awake at night wondering if your job is on the list. Even if it's not, knowing that Kent's job *is* might leave you with a guilt knot in your stomach for days.

There's also a chance that the boss will walk in as Marcia is mid-sentence in a balking marathon—in which case you're guilty by association. It'll look like you're having a conversation about the boss even if you're just acting as a sounding board.

If you think you can just offer an ear to bend without getting caught up in the company gossip or top-secret memos, offer to take Marcia to lunch. There's little chance the boss will walk in, and you'll have a friend at the front desk to calm down that client when he comes in to yell at you!

℘ Speaking of receptionists . . .

Secretary's Day, now officially called "Administrative Professional's Day," traditionally falls between April 21 and 25. If you have an assistant, check out the following great websites. If you are an assistant, drop this list on your boss's desk.

Looking for a great card for the person who does everything? Try cardblvd.com/secretariesz.htm.

How about an original balloon bouquet with messages that tell her how special you think she is from usflowercompany.com?

No one can resist the candy mug gift pack! Find it at http://baskets4u.com/secretary.htm.

Want a poem that really speaks your mind? Print out the "Ode to Secretaries" at homesweetbusiness.com/gallery/appreciation.htm.

Fun Factoid

If you're a secretary, you're in good company! In 1996, the United States had 3.2 million secretaries, down from 3.9 million in 1983, the earliest year for which comparable data are available. (**Source:** census.gov/Press-Release/cb97-199.html)

78

The Trekkie Techie

Use your people skills to make
the geeky computer tech an ally.

*"To err is human, but to really foul things up
requires a computer."*
—Anonymous

You have to love technology. Only in the twenty-first century can
you conduct international banking, send your best buddy on
another continent an instant message, and learn just about anything
under the sun with the high-tech gizmos found on practically every
desk in the country. But when your gizmo has a glitch, who are you
gonna call? Most likely, you'll be forced to turn to the company techie
for help if you want to get out of the ditch of a dead blank screen to
screamin' back down the information superhighway.

Most company techies are perfectly pleasant when it comes to res-
cuing technologically challenged coworkers stuck in computing pur-
gatory. Pardon our perpetuating a stereotype (after all, every industry
has its goofballs), but some techies are maladjusted geniuses who prefer to serve you a side of ill-mannered scorn and ridicule for interrupting their day with your inept computer skills. Does the following
sound familiar?

You: "Could you fix my computer? It froze up while I was trying to
download a file."

Techie: "Don't know how to force it to restart?" (frowns with look of disgust) "How big a file was it?"

You: "Um, I dunno. Six megs or gigs or something that ended with 'ig.'"

Techie: "You tried downloading a six gig file with a 32K modem?" (no longer trying to hide his contempt) "Duh! No wonder it froze!"

You: "Sorry, the only number and letter combination I understand is 14K."

If this sounds like your company's computer geek, you may be better off than you think. Spending hours hunched in front of a monitor avoiding daylight may not have done much to further your techie's people skills, but his or her gigantic brain is yours for the picking! With a little finesse and flattery, get the techie to show you how to reboot (or anything else that you might need) yourself, and explain any other computer-related conundrums while he or she is at it. Techies consider it a compliment that you show an interest in their field, and you may pick up some priceless skills to boot. Any computer knowledge, even if it's a few magic keystroke shortcuts, will make your life easier and may just impress your boss when you are asked to come to the rescue of the boss's fried hard drive.

So you chatted up the techie about modems and hard drives. Now what? Now you have a name to add as a resource for future computer trouble. If the techie is approachable, shoot him or her an E-mail with your hardware or software stumpers. People outside the company pay $100 an hour or more for the expertise of techies-for-hire: there's no rule that says you can't mooch a few free pointers.

All this talk about technology might make you want to learn more about computers in order to be a techie yourself someday. Then you can look through your bottle-cap glasses down your nose at the other poor technologically challenged people.

✎ Speaking of techies . . .

Powerful female CEOs exist in the top echelon of high-tech companies. CEO Carly Fiorina heads up Hewlett-Packard and Compaq. Lucent Technologies is run by female CEO Patricia Russo, while Anne Mulcahy is president of Xerox. High-tech company Software Spectrum is headed by CEO Judy Odom, while Cinda Hallman heads up Spherion.

A recommended techie tome: to bone up on technical terms without falling asleep, pick up a copy of *Windows for Dummies*.

79

I'm Rubber and You're Glue

Deflect a coworker's verbal attack.

"I've had a good time, but this wasn't it."
—Groucho Marx

You know how you always think of the perfect comeback several hours *after* someone has insulted you? It's so frustrating, especially if you can't go back later to discuss the matter—like with strangers and past clients.

With coworkers, however, you *do* have the opportunity to return to the scene of the crime—or at least to the perpetrator's office.

The trick, of course, is to know just what to say to make your point (without using any cuss words or throwing paperweights).

Here are a few ideas for getting to the heart of the matter while maintaining your cool (and dignity).

Ask the person what his or her intention was. It's highly doubtful that he or she will say, "I was trying to hurt your feelings" or "To make you look stupid." More likely, the offender will stumble around for a phrase that makes it look like he or she was trying to help you. "Well, Jane, I was just trying to point out the fact that you should be careful in your conversations with clients." If this is the case, you'll want to point out other ways to get the point across in the future, such as "Well, John, I understand your concern, but you should know that I'm actually quite approachable and open to criticism in a constructive manner. Perhaps next time instead of raising your voice you could approach me in private and explain in detail how I could have better dealt with our client."

Saying, "What is your intention in telling me this?" also works well on the spot. It will not only catch the person off guard, but may cause the offender to rethink his or her approach.

Another idea is to lead by example. When you have an issue with coworkers, treat them as you would like to be treated. Pull them aside and use language that expresses your concern while allowing them to give examples of how they will better handle the situation next time. Be clear on why their actions were inappropriate instead of just accusing them of wrongdoing.

If you feel that you must defend or explain your actions when you are verbally attacked, do so in a private setting to avoid attracting the attention of other employees. "Melissa, we seem to have some discrepancies on this issue. Why don't we go into your office to work them out in private?"

Once you've secured privacy, replay your actions and intentions to let Melissa know that you were not purposely attempting to harm the company or its relationship with a client.

Try to understand the other person's view. By putting yourself in the perpetrator's shoes, you may be able to more fully understand his concern. This may allow you to validate his feelings without coming across as defensive. "Jason, I can see why you'd be concerned that I might be sharing company secrets. The information that you received would lead me to the same conclusion. Fortunately, you've been misinformed. Here's what *really* happened . . ."

By clarifying the facts without using language that implies Jason is lying, you let him off the hook to further understand the truth.

Taking the time to better communicate with your coworkers will make everyone's job easier, and no one will have to feel like he or she is walking on eggshells to avoid a fight.

80

Pleading the Fifth

Respond to coworker dishonesty with discretion.

"I get so tired listening to one million dollars here, one million dollars there. It's so petty."
—Imelda Marcos, on her embezzlement trial

You're a good person, or try to be. You offer the last free taxi to the old lady next to you on the street (unless you're late for a date), never cheat on your taxes (cheating and reporting the numbers optimistically are different), and always try to be friendly when in public, especially to the chiseled-jaw types. So, surely you've never stolen anything from work, right? Hey, it's not your fault they choose those fine-point blue Bics you love writing with, then leave a giant box of them unattended in the supply room to tempt you!

From snagging a stray paperclip to embezzling yacht-loads of cash and indulging in insider trading, a surprising amount of dishonesty on the job exists. It seems that when it comes to defining honesty, many of us wouldn't be caught dead hot-wiring a car. Yet admittedly, some of us feel it's no big deal to swipe a pen or desk calendar that the Big Faceless Corporation won't miss anyway (rationalized by the fact that if the company can't give you the pay raise you deserve, it can afford a free stapler now and then).

But what if the stolen shoe is on the other foot, namely that of a coworker? What should you do if you work in a clothing store and see a coworker smuggling sweaters out under her coat? What about catching a colleague "co-opting" computer supplies? It's a tough call. After all, stealing is wrong, and you should, as your mama would say, "do the right thing." On the other hand, nobody likes a whistleblower.

Say you stumble in and catch someone in stealus interruptus and he freezes. Try saying, "Sorry, but I just saw that." It puts the awkward moment on the offender and gives him a chance to put the loot down and walk away. It also gives you a chance to "un-see" whatever you saw. If he's smart, he'll mumble something unintelligible, put it down, and scurry off, never to mention it again.

But a brasher burglar may walk off anyway, assuming you won't tell. You can tattle, but be prepared for some unexpected consequences. Not only could the perpetrator deny it and set off an ugly his-word-against-yours scenario, but managers may be surprisingly unappreciative that you've designated yourself the company cop. Try being direct and saying, "Hey, you thief, you're making me uncomfortable." You don't involve the manager this way, and the person has a chance to save face.

Need another way to deal with it? HR people are good at saying, "My door is always open." Test that theory by plopping down in the person's office and blabbing the details of what happened. Chances are the HR rep has run into a similar situation, or will know where to take the beans once you've spilled them.

If you want to wimp out and choose a more surreptitious solution, try dropping a note in the company suggestion box. Jot some thing nonaccusatory, like "put security measures in employee break room to cut down on internal theft" rather than "Susie's sticky fingers keep walking off with inventory when she closes shop," and count on managers to get the drift from there.

Just remember to give your coworkers the benefit of the doubt in these situations. After all, where'd you get that pad of sticky notes you keep next to your phone at home?

81

Power to the People

Use key phrases to make a strong point.

"Wit is educated insolence."
—**Aristotle**

Unlike men, women don't need to take over small third world countries just to make a point. We actually have a blood supply that can run to *two* parts of our body at the same time (in this case, the brain and the mouth).

The problem is, the fact that we're intelligent doesn't mean people always hear what we're saying. It's often frustrating to try to get our great ideas across when our intended audience is zoning out.

The key is to use effective phrasing that will catch the "listener's" attention. Here are a few ideas to get you started.

When it comes to presenting an idea to the head honcho, be it male or female, everything comes down to the bottom line. The decision makers need to know (1) how much it will cost them to implement your idea and (2) how much money they'll make when it's finished. Use phrases like "Our investment will be minimal" and "As you can see, our profit will far outweigh our contribution." By avoiding the word *cost*, the CEO, CFO, and Johnny Naysayer may be more likely to view the company's financial input merely as investment from which they'll see a hefty return. You may also want to mention a time line in order to show that you've done your homework. Terms like "return on investment by May of next year" will demonstrate that the idea could bring a nearly immediate profit to the company.

Terms that show off your thoroughness are sure to impress your target audience. "I've researched back to 1990 and compiled a list of our top twenty biggest clients" is an indication that you're not only serious, but careful to cover all your bases. Likewise with presenting a "worst-case scenario." Although no one wants to hear bad projections, it shows that you won't be caught off guard if the plan fails to succeed for any reason. This is important, as no plan is foolproof. It will also protect you when Johnny Naysayer starts throwing alternate scenarios at you in front of the entire Board of Directors.

There's more to life than money, and even the stingiest tightwad knows that sometimes nonmonetary benefits can lead to monetary benefits. Be sure to include key phrases like "increased visibility" and "value-added service" to demonstrate that your idea can help the company grow and increase its clients' satisfaction.

Dropping names is often considered tacky in the business world. Not so in your presentation. If you can cite examples (the more famous the better!) or add validation to your idea by mentioning other employees who have contributed to the project, do so. Without giving away all the credit, let your listeners know that other people are already on board. "Jason from finance said that our clients are frequently asking for ways to cut down on their paperwork." Even if you *are* the sole brains behind the proposal, offer a few examples of how the idea has already worked. "When VoiceStream wireless took on Jamie Lee Curtis as its spokesperson, its revenue increased by 30 percent." Be careful not to mention any employees who *haven't* given you permission to include them. Many people are quick to jump on board as a contributor if the proposal is a success, but if it bombs, they'll pretend they weren't involved. Call them fair-weather friends. It's a power phrase that's sure to return as you continue to pitch the many ideas you have percolating in that nonstop brain of yours. Can you say "overtime"?

82

When the COBRA Strikes

Opt for COBRA health insurance coverage
when you quit your job.

No matter who you are, being healthy, wealthy, and wise is about the best a gal could hope for. If you've been blessed with good health your whole life, it's easy to take it for granted . . . until you're sidelined with the flu or some minor malady that makes you think, "I promise I'll never take my health for granted again!"

The bad news is, even if you think you're healthy as a horse, going without health insurance is *indeed* taking your health for granted. And if you have some sort of recurring illness, it's just plain dumb. Who's going to remove your appendix when it flares up, or put your broken leg in a cast when you fall off your bike? "Oh, the hospital will fix me up," you reason. "They're not going to let me croak on their doorstep." That's probably true, but paying for even a minor injury out-of-pocket means parting with thousands of dollars or being forced to declare bankruptcy to avoid payment. Talk about a major headache (which you won't be able to see the doctor for because you have no insurance!).

The good news is, you never have to be without insurance—even if you quit your job or get fired! Under the stuffy-sounding but very handy federal Consolidated Omnibus Budget Reconciliation Act

(COBRA for short), all employees can keep their company-sponsored health insurance for up to eighteen months after they leave their job, even for their dependents! All they have to do is pay the premium, plus a 2 percent administration fee for the paperwork.

Why should you care, if you never plan on being unemployed? Because you never know when you may be in an accident (that's why they're called accidents!) or your job will end suddenly. Maybe in two years you'll become disillusioned with corporate life, leaving your former yuppie self behind as you take off to live in a VW van for a year on the beach. Bohemians need coverage, too—you never know when you'll get a nasty hemp-related rash that demands medical attention.

Or, perhaps you'll decide to take off and start your own company someday. You have big dreams of having a huge staff under your command, but most likely, it'll just be you in the beginning. Electing to continue your COBRA coverage, rather than wrangle with getting your own independent insurance, means minimal fuss and uninterrupted coverage. Hey, why waste time jumping through health insurance hoops, when you could be plotting your business strategy in your quest for corporate world domination? COBRA comes in handy, especially if you have a chronic condition, need medication, and aren't up for the hassles involved in preexisting condition clauses.

Then there's the other benefit to COBRA coverage—peace of mind. It's a bummer to be between jobs, but too scared to indulge in sports or other risky pursuits. Get COBRA coverage just in case. Then, when your friends call and suggest an afternoon of skydiving, you can say, "Jumping out of a plane at ten thousand feet? I am *so* there!"

For More Information

Want more info on COBRA? Check out dol.gov/pwba/pubs/cobrafs.htm. For info on COBRA coverage during divorce, go to divorceinfo.com/cobra.htm.

83

Please Pass the Project

Enlighten the company slacker.

"Enemies are so stimulating."
—**Katharine Hepburn**

$\mathcal{S}$ eeing as you're a "company girl" poster child, you probably won't believe this, but some people don't like doing work. And as someone who's used to working alone you're in for a shocker with your first attempt at a group project. Here it is: some people don't pull their weight.

Yes, you heard it here first: there are people out there who don't want to work but still want to get credit for it. Yes, we know—it's a horrible concept, but that's why they're called *slackers*. By not pulling their weight, they let the rope slack.

You'll know who the person in your group is (let's hope there's only one!) before the first meeting is over. Slackers will come up with lots of great ideas but then expect someone else to implement them. They'll probably recommend committees (to ensure the work gets accomplished) but then refuse (or conveniently "forget") to sign up for one. They may announce that they'll be doing "tons of research until the next meeting," which will make them *appear* busy, but most likely you'll later learn that they (1) already had all of the statistics before the project even started or (2) had their assistant gather all the information.

Granted, slackers aren't always easy to spot. The more advanced life-forms have evolved to blend in with their surroundings—looking busy at a moment's notice. Over time they've developed the concentrating scowl (complete with furrowed brow and intent stare) and mastered the fast-paced scuffle that one might see on an overloaded lawyer late for court.

Still, there are tricks for flushing the slacker out of his or her foxhole. If you're in a position of authority, delegation can be a very powerful weapon. "Mike, I'm going to need you to get me the last three years' tax returns, including files on our ten biggest clients each year." A slacker will have an excuse forming on his lips before you can even finish your sentence. If he doesn't, it may be because he's already drafting a note to his receptionist. You can solve this problem by making sure his receptionist is not only busy with her own assignments, but also well aware that she is not to help her boss with this project no matter how hard he pushes. "And Shannon, I realize that you're already busy with Mike's everyday tasks, but I could really use your research skills. Can you focus on getting me some information on court cases relating to incorporated taxes?"

If Shannon's as smart as she appears, she'll know exactly what you're doing and will be grateful for it. She has her eye on Mike's job, and she knows there's no room for slackers in the corner office.

On the other hand, if you're not in a position to delegate to Mike, you'll need to divide the work on a project *in front of other people*—preferably, your supervisor. This can be done during a meeting if it's a quick, general division, such as "Great. Perhaps the best way to start is for me to set up meetings with each of our clients. Mike, while I'm doing that, can you pull all their files and determine who our largest clients are?" This will put Mike on the spot—leaving him to confirm that he'll do it or suggest another option. If he's a true slacker, be prepared for the latter. If Mike's new suggestion seems unfair, address it immediately—in front of other people. "That's certainly a viable option, Mike. However, I'm concerned that my assignment may take four times as long as yours. This wouldn't be fair to you as you'd have to do all the other work. How about . . . (enter option number three)."

If you still can't come to an agreement, the meeting may need to move on. If this is the case, ask a neutral third party to stay after the meeting. "John, do you think you could stay and help us figure out the best plan of action to complete this project efficiently, fairly, and effectively?" Most likely, John has worked with Mike before or will at least take the hint that you need an ally.

Just be sure that as the project deadline nears, Mike is completing his share of the work. If not, you'll need to confront him and/or his superior. He may be a slacker, but you have your eye on a promotion. Your boss needs to know that you're deserving for your hard work—and for putting up with Mike.

84

Ousting Overtime

Work forty action-packed hours to avoid overtime.

"I must govern the clock, not be governed by it."
—**Golda Meir**

Is your once easy, enjoyable job becoming like the song "Working in a Coal Mine," sunup to sundown? Does leaving on time sound like an impossible dream? Maybe you need to brush up on your "work smarter, not harder" (and not longer!) skills and squeeze more work out of work, rather than letting work squeeze more life out of you.

It's no surprise that bosses demand more from us than ever before. In fact, the average North American works almost 20 percent more hours on average than workers did just thirty years ago. In these days of downsizing, multitasking, and bending over backward to keep Big Boss Man happy with our performance, it's easy to see why we all work longer hours. But while we can't control time, we can be smart about where we spend our time and keep overtime to a minimum.

How? With excellent and easy time management techniques, that's how! Finding out where your time is being spent (and possibly wasted) is the best way to magically find a few extra hours in the day.

First, keep a log of how you spend your time during the day. Be honest: if you really do spend forty-five minutes gossiping with the receptionist, making coffee, and E-mailing jokes to your friends, write it down. Monitor your time for one week and see where your minutes need better managing. You may be amazed to find you waste a good chunk of hours surfing the Internet. Sure surfing's fun, but getting a big report done with that chunk may mean the difference between breezing out at 5:30 P.M. and toiling away till 8:00 P.M. on a Friday night.

Note your personal "up" times while you're at it. Are you at your peppiest prelunch, and do you feel like a decrepit old slug from three to five? Plan to tackle high-priority tasks during your up times and leave lowly chores for slack time. So, what's high priority? Check your daily to-do list (You *do* have a daily to-do list, don't you?) and number the items. Scads of experts swear that simply writing tasks down vastly improves the possibility of those tasks getting tackled.

Time management mavens also swear by "time blocking" as an effective way to get more done in less time. Time blocking means setting aside certain times to do routine tasks like answering voice mail and checking E-mail—and messing with these chores only during those set times. Every time you stop midproject because your voice mail light is flashing means taking time to refocus on the task at hand.

It's challenging enough to handle your own job. Don't inadvertently handle someone else's job for him or her. Have a clueless coworker who's always pestering you for help? Showing your coworker how to log on, explaining company procedures, and other hand-holding is awfully nice of you, but it takes precious time away from your work (and your free time, if your schedule creeps into overtime). Come to coworkers' aid, but make it quick. Better yet, refer them to their manager, who gets paid to train and mentor them.

Speaking of overtime . . .

Overtime is based on a forty-hour workweek, not an eight-hour day. The Federal Fair Labor Standards Act (FLSA) requires certain employers to pay one and a half times the regular rate of wages for hours over forty in a workweek.

85

Beggars Can't Be Choosers

Cope with the codependent coworker
who's constantly trying to bum from you.

*"Some cause happiness wherever they go;
others, whenever they go."*
—Oscar Wilde

The codependent coworker, whether male or female, is always annoying. Requests range from "bumming a ride" to "borrowing" something with no intention of ever giving it back. Items that fall under the latter category include cigarettes, cigars, gum, candy, beverages, and virtually any other food item.

Perhaps the worst the office beggar can do to annoy his or her coworkers is to ask to borrow money. No one likes to lend money to friends, let alone someone you only know from staff meetings and memo routing slips. So how does one address such an annoying and persistent coworker?

The first thing to do is hide your personal items: makeup, food, cigarettes, lotion, whatever—keep it out of sight. If by chance your "Please, sir, may I have some more?" buddy catches you midapplication with a tube of lipstick, just explain that you're really not comfortable sharing items that touch your mouth.

If the item in question doesn't pose a sanitary problem, consider the poverty-stricken guilt trip. "Well, John, I'll give you this one cookie, but that's it. I'm on a really tight budget, and unless you can swing me a huge raise, the cookies are on you next time."

If this *is* next time, don't be afraid to remind John about the last time he asked for a cookie. "You know, John, I think it may be time for you to ask for a raise. I know it's bad when I'm paying for your snacks with my measly salary. I think I mentioned last time that the cookies were on you." Sure, this may be embarrassing for you, as it implies that you can't afford to give away a cookie, but more likely it'll be embarrassing to John, who can't even afford to buy his own cookies.

As for the rides home, your response will depend on your situation. If it's out of your way, feel free to say so. If you feel obligated, don't be embarrassed to ask for gas money. (This may also cut down on the number of times you're asked to give rides.)

If it's on your way but you just don't want to get stuck in traffic with Willy the Whiner or Tammy the Talker, make an excuse ("Sorry, I'm heading out to a friend's house") or sneak out the back door before you can get cornered. You could always hide in the bathroom until Willy finds another ride—but there's a chance you may get stuck in there with Tammy—and she's short on funds this week.

86

Pulling a Clark Kent

To get out of work mode fast,
change clothes before you leave work.

*"When work is a pleasure, life is a joy!
When work is duty, life is slavery."*
—**Maxim Gorky**

What do you wear when you're not at work? Whether you're a diehard holey jeans and tank-topped slob, or have a closet the size of the first floor at Nordstrom, chances are your work wardrobe is just that—your work wardrobe. The typical working woman's cushy insoled shoes, Dockers-style slacks, and stretchy shirts are casual enough, but not exactly super comfortable. After all, how many people do you see kicking around the park on a Saturday afternoon in panty hose and pumps?

Plenty of us just plain don't like dressing up for work and don't have the bucks to buy two wardrobes. You may have to spend all day in boring beige tweed, secretly denying your leather-clad and halter topped true self, but you don't have to spend all night in beigeland, too! Bring a set of togs to work and see how a simple change of clothes can mean a total change in attitude.

Why bother, you say? Why waste time and energy hauling another set of clothes around with you? There are plenty of positives to changing before you leave work. You may spend a summer day toiling in an air-conditioned environment that's positively frosty, only to spend an hour's drive home in a blistering hot car. Had you thrown a simple shorts and T-shirt in the back seat before ripping out of the driveway, you could be working on your tan (at least on your driver's-side arm, anyway) rather than cursing that plastic bag feeling from your polyester-blend blouse.

Plus, work clothes usually cost a pretty penny. The sooner you get out of them the less wear, tear, sweat, and ketchup stains result. Spilling an after-work strawberry smoothie on yourself is decidedly less tragic when your faded "1994 Blues Festival" T-shirt, rather than your best silk vest, is the target.

And think of all the time changing right after work can save you! Whether you're heading to the gym, a softball game, the grocery store, or your best friend's house, you'll get to skip stopping by your apartment and scrounging up something to wear. You could always wear your work clothes wherever you go after work . . . if you wanted to look like a yuppie dork, that is. It's a little hard to relax when your "corporate stiff" outfit doesn't jive with your "kicked back and chillin' " inner self.

But the best reason of all to bring spare stuff is the mental shift that accompanies shedding your work attire. Ditch those crabby customers, shifty sales managers, and other job-related hassles along with your dirty socks! If you waitress, weld, or work around smells, this is especially important. It's a little hard to leave your workday behind when you're walking around smelling like you're still there.

⌐⊙ Work Wardrobe? Make Mine Stripes.

U.S. Army General Claudia Kennedy, who retired in June of 2001, was the Deputy Chief of Staff for Intelligence and a three-star general in the United States Army, the first and only woman to ever achieve this rank.

87

ſticking to Your Guns

Leave work at 5 P.M. without feeling guilty.

> *"Show me a woman who doesn't feel guilty,*
> *and I'll show you a man."*
> —**Erica Jong**

Maybe you're going out of town. Or perhaps your parents are arriving with only a few hours' notice and your place is a mess. Or maybe you completely forgot about those very expensive tickets to the opera that are for tonight and you still don't have a dress? It doesn't matter what your reason. You've put in your eight hours, and now it's time to leave work at work. Don't let your coworker sucker you (or guilt you!) into staying late. You pride yourself on maximum efficiency at work, and leaving on time is your reward.

Let's say there's a project-passer looking for his own easy way out by 5 P.M. Most everyone else has left, and he's looking for you.

Depending on how your office is set up, you'll have the obvious escape routes: the bathroom window, the back door, or the break room's Secret Smoker door. You know, the one where Prissy Pauline declares that she's taking out the trash because it's full of coffee grounds but takes five minutes to walk back from the dumpster.

If you're on a higher floor or don't have any other exits that don't sound an alarm, you'll need to be more creative.

If you do end up running into the project-passer, start with the direct approach. "Sorry, John. I'm on my way out. Good luck with the project and have a great weekend." Usually, if you say this as you're walking away, there's little chance for rebuttal. The project-passer will be so busy turning to try to find someone else before everyone leaves that he'll keep from following you out to the parking lot. You can walk away knowing you were honest and assertive.

When straight honesty doesn't work, there's always the little white lie. Feign a meeting. "Sorry, John. I'm meeting someone at 5:30 P.M. and I can't be late." You don't need to go into any details about who you're meeting, why you're meeting, and especially *where* you're meeting. The last thing you want is for John to invite himself along. "Oh, you're meeting Sam at that little sports bar down the street? Great. I love that place!"

This doesn't actually have to be a lie if you're planning on seeing a human later in the night; a husband, boyfriend, child, friend, roommate, or even pizza delivery person makes the "meeting" all the more real.

If all else fails, offer to help on the next business day. "John, I'd love to help you, but I can't tonight. I'd be happy to assist you on Monday. If that's too late, I suggest you contact the boss and let her know you're behind. Maybe she'll let you have an extension."

John may appreciate your suggestion and feel some sort of relief at the possibility that he'll have more time to complete the work. If he scoffs at your idea, don't take it personally. It probably means that this deadline *was* an extension, in which case John may not *be* there on Monday.

Did you know . . .

Ballpoint ink is dye dissolved in vegetable oils and/or castor oil? (**Source:** http://vigilanteventures.com/trivia/office)

88

Timing Is Everything

Order dinner before you leave work so it
arrives at your house the same time you do.

"Life itself is the proper binge."
—Julia Child

Ah . . . finally off work and you're sitting at the umpteenth stop-light when it hits you—hey, you're hungry! Eight hours spent corporate raiding (or slinging beers or ringing up grouchy shoppers or whatever you do to earn a buck) can work up quite a hunger.

Suddenly you remember: the only edible food at home is a crusty rack of empty condiment jars and something covered with fur that looks like Chia bologna. But the thought of fighting the grocery store crowds is simply painful, as is running to the drive-through for yet another McWhatever.

This dilemma can be solved with two beautiful words: restaurant delivery.

Not only could you be eating a fabulous meal that's blissfully not home cooked, with a little strategic planning you could time the delivery just right. All you need is a cell phone and a few takeout menus or pizza flyers cleverly stashed in your glove compartment or scribbled from the office yellow pages beforehand.

Just call in your order on the way home, and you'll hopefully time the delivery perfectly. It's an art, really. Call in too late and you'll be forced to pick through your bare larder in search of an appetizer, fruit-lessly opening and slamming cabinets as you mutter, "There's never anything to eat in this stupid house." However, call in too soon and you'll leave some poor guy hard up for his dollar tip with a bag full of moo goo gai pan forlornly standing on your stoop, pounding on your door in vain, and risk being labeled a prank orderer.

To avert disaster, communicate with order takers and tell them flat out, "I'm ten minutes away" so they'll help time it from their end. Heck, get on a first-name basis and tip well, and you'll get the expec-tant delivery boy circling the block on your behalf in anticipation of your arrival.

Stuck in traffic and have visions of your pepperoni getting cold and a pouting delivery boy cursing your name? Think fast! Call the restau-rant back and tell the dispatcher you've been delayed. He or she can postpone your order or have the delivery person deliver other orders before yours. Or, see if the restaurant can accept your credit card over the phone (plus tip) and leave the order on your doorstep. If all else fails, pick a restaurant nearby: you can swing by and pick up what they think is a bogus order.

No cell phone? No problem! Call in your order just as you're walk-ing out the door at work. It goes without saying you'll need to guessti-mate your food's ETA versus your estimated commuter time.

If you don't feel like eating restaurant food, try this idea with your neighborhood grocery store. Some neighborhood joints and mom-and-pop corner stores offer delivery. This offers healthier choices, along with well-deserved beer and wine.

Hot food delivered right to your door after a hard day's work is sort of like manna (or sweet-and-sour pork, depending on what you ordered) from heaven.

89

The Penny-Pincher

Try these money-saving tips for the tight budget.

> *"People who are always making allowance for themselves soon go bankrupt."*
> —**Mary Pettibone Poole**

If you've been trying to motivate yourself to do some spring cleaning, you now have the perfect excuse. Lift up those couch cushions and revel in the miracle that poverty-stricken smarties call the "Jackpot": loose change limbo.

Although the nickels and dimes may not seem like much to the unknowing Fat Cat, even the copper coins will come in handy to the woman who knows how to make every penny count.

Let's start with food. The golden rule is brown bagging, of course. Even the CEO is wasting her money by eating out every day. Still, there are times when someone else's cooking is best. (No, we're not advocating that you steal your coworkers' sandwiches from the staff lounge fridge!) The idea is to convince your coworkers to split up the lunch responsibilities. Bring a tray of lasagna on Monday and share it with four of your coworkers. Then have a different person bring the group meal each day Tuesday through Friday. You're only cooking one day, and you have five different dishes to sample during the week. (Now isn't that better than a tuna sandwich every day?)

There's one precaution, however. You don't want to learn at 11:45 A.M. that Susie has called in sick when it's her day to bring lunch. If you're down to your last dollar, you could end up snacking on a Snickers bar, and although the company's slogan is "Snickers really satisfies," it doesn't say for how long. By 3 P.M. you may be biting your nails for nourishment.

After work, some happy hours also offer free buffets. The food isn't always glamorous—a giant hoagie, chicken wings, or egg rolls—but you may be able to fill up on finger food as your coworkers chug down a few beers.

If you live close enough to work, you can also save some money by walking, riding your bike, or taking the bus. Many public transportation systems now offer discount bus or subway fare packages for a flat fee. A yearly fee of $100 for unlimited use will be more than offset by the cost of gas you'd otherwise be spending on your commute. Not to mention that you'll be saving the environment from yet another vehicle's emissions.

Carpooling is a good option if you live too far from work to walk or if you're not on a bus route. Take a poll (of the coworkers you like!) and find out who lives in your part of town. Be prepared to list the advantages (better for the environment, less lonely ride, saving on gas, shorter commute since you'll be in the fast-moving carpool lane!) in order to convince the hard sells.

Although penny-pinching may impress your girlfriends, you may want to be careful who you tell about your bargain tips. First of all, you don't want to come across as cheap. That hottie on the ninth floor will never ask you out if he hears you're living on tomato soup (ketchup in hot water). In addition, you don't want to give away all your trade secrets. It only takes one glutton to ruin the free buffet. Have you forgotten the company picnic already?

And you had come prepared with all those freezer bags . . .

90

Prescheduled Pamper Time

Schedule an after-work massage or manicure
for an end-of-the-day pick-me-up.

"Can one desire too much of a good thing?"
—Shakespeare

Pop quiz. It's five o'clock and stress has you feeling stretched tighter
than a Pam Anderson tube top. What to do?

A. Veer off the freeway into the nearest tacky tavern and booze
   up, not stopping till your IQ plummets to meet your rapidly
   increasing blood alcohol concentration.
B. Lie on the couch with a box of doughnuts and eat them until
   you actually feel another chin grow.
C. Indulge yourself in a stress-releasing pamper time to wash
   every last work-related molecule of angst from your psyche.

Did you pick C? Good for you! You've obviously figured out that C
is the healthiest choice.

Indulging in an after-work massage, pedicure, or other personal
pamper treatment serves two purposes, really. Not only does it help
erase the wear and tear already done to your attitude, heart rate, or
tootsies, it signals your brain, "Hey, work is over. Now it's me time."
Experts and working women everywhere insist it's not even the pam-

pering primarily that feels so darn good, but the ritual of a regular break that's so beneficial.

If you have money, honey, schedule a standing appointment on a Friday afternoon with a masseuse whose fingers simply walk on water. You'll feel good knowing it's already set up, and it'll give you something to look forward to, plus cut down the possibility you'll talk yourself out of spending the time and money on yourself. A pedicure or manicure works just as well for you high-maintenance chicks who don't feel like disrobing just to get your groove back.

No money is no problem, either. Dust off that gym lifetime membership card and see if that spa has a sauna or hot tub. If so, throw a suit and towel in your trunk and every Friday, stop by the spa and roast your body. You might even feel compelled to throw a sit-up or two in while you're there. Few things melt away stress faster than sweating through every pore in your body. You'll know you're done when your spine's left with all the rigidity of a wrung-out dishrag.

More ideas that don't involve a gym card include making a beeline for the bathtub (past the mailbox and answering machine, mind you) for a hot, free soak. Just do your aching feet if you don't want to douse your whole self.

Or, stop by your corner bookstore or library and plop down in a chair near the magazine rack. It doesn't get any cheaper or quieter than free issues of *Architectural Digest* in a window seat. Arrive preoccupied with your boss's bitching, leave with fantasies of a hand-painted cupola Italian ceiling dancing in your head.

Just pick something pampering that says, "I'm spoiled" that's also personal. Get your palm read. Bash balls at a driving range, go smoke a stogie in the park, or shoot pinball at the local arcade. How often? Not so much that it becomes routine, but regularly enough to signal "stress relief" to your system.

91

You're Breaking Up

Squelch cell phone interruptions.

> *"The nice thing about egotists is that they don't talk about other people."*
> —Lucille S. Harper

At the movies. During sex. Mid-funeral.

What do all these things have in common? They are all inappropriate times for your cell phone to ring.

OK. So you already know the *obvious* ones, but what about the times when you can't turn it off for fear of missing an important call, but know you should? Staff meetings, corporate functions, and even children's recitals can make for embarrassing situations if the call does happen to come in. Luckily, there are solutions.

Let voice mail pick up. If you don't have voice mail on your cell phone, get it or have the calls redirected to your office where you can call in for messages later. Whenever possible, call the person you need to speak with and explain that you won't be available after all. Offer another time to call or suggest that you call him or her back later.

Schedule your time in advance. You may be saying, "But I have to work around my *clients'* schedule—be available to them in case they want to close the big deal!" Not true. Any client worth working with will probably not only be willing to work with you, but may actually respect your commitment. Clients may even be impressed that you're committed to seeing your daughter's piano recital or son's first football game without interruptions or that you respect *their* time enough to give them your undivided attention. Besides, you don't want to look desperate.

Tell your coworkers that you're expecting an important call from a client before the meeting starts. By letting them know ahead of time, you can simply excuse yourself from the meeting without getting dirty looks.

Change your ring. Many cell phones now offer a silent vibration instead of a ring. If your phone doesn't already offer the option, consider switching phones for one that does.

Prepare in advance. If you absolutely must take the call, sit near an exit so you can quickly excuse yourself without bothering other attendees. Make the call short by offering to call back at a later time if you have to.

Unfortunately, many "no call" lists do not apply to business or cell phone numbers. Leave a voice mail telling telemarketers to remove your name from their calling list, or tell them if you answer the call yourself. If someone else frequently answers your cell phone, give him or her permission to do the same. It may cut back on the number of telemarketing calls you receive and will offer you some peace of mind as you listen to Vivaldi's Concerto in D Minor.

92

How Am I Doing?

Make the most of a good quarterly review—
or survive a crappy one.

*"The thing women have got to learn is that
nobody gives you power. You just take it."*
—Roseanne

The annual review: it's a necessary evil to monitor workers and inform them of their progress. Though most workers dread the experience, a performance review is a golden opportunity to pitch for a raise, a promotion, that corner office, or at least for a chance to see how your boss thinks you're doing and how you could improve. But if you're like most workers, you look forward to this angst-inducing lesson in humility about as much as an emergency root canal performed by a dentist with shaky hands.

Are you the type of chick who actually looks forward to your boss's unflinching feedback when you ask her if you're doing a good job? Good for you. Chances are you *are* doing a good job, or you wouldn't be putting yourself out there like that. But since even star employees can shine even brighter, your boss will likely point out a few areas you could improve on. Are you "punctuality challenged" in the mornings? Have your sales slouched lately? Have you missed a few key deadlines? Pay attention to what your boss points out rather than immediately forming your verbal defense in your head. Don't forget to ask him or her for specific advice on how to improve your performance.

Maybe you think you'll get dinged for heading out early some Fridays, but your boss only mentions your atrocious spelling in company memos. Knowing exactly what hoops Mr. Boss Man wants you to jump through will spell out your game plan, rather than leave you foggily fighting for a vague notion of how to get ahead.

When your manager's monologue ends is when your response begins, so don't begin by being defensive or overly emotional. Bosses like solutions, and responding honestly but succinctly and with a minimum amount of whining will get you far. Blowing your top and fleeing the room in tears will not.

Have fabulous rapport with the boss and get a swell review? Great! Now's the time to talk about what's on your mind. Want to know how to get ahead? Want a promotion? Want to pitch a four-day workweek? There's no better time than the present, and a great review gives you the much-needed leverage to finagle a few perks for yourself. Companies love happy, productive employees and will want to please you.

If the review's going really bad and you're on the brink of blowing your cool, simply say, "Could you excuse me for a minute?" and go cool your jets in the ladies' room (your boss will just assume you had one too many large iced teas).

Stop the meeting if you feel the urge to blurt out, "This godforsaken job is sucking the very life out of me" or "This isn't worth it. I quit!" Instead, say, "You've given me a lot to think about. I'd like to think about this before I respond. Can we continue this meeting tomorrow?" This allows you crucial cooling down time.

Then, you can whistle the melody to "Take This Job and Shove It" all the way back to your desk. That, rather than exploding, will ensure you have a desk to go back to.

93

Let Her Rip!

Use tact when complaining about a coworker.

"The reason there are so few female politicians is that
it is too much trouble to put makeup on two faces."
—Maureen Murphy

Complaining about a coworker is always easy. It's doing it tactfully that's so difficult.

Because there's a great deal of risk involved in bitching to a boss, it's best to do so only as a last resort. Your first attempt should always be to talk with the person. Confront coworkers on the spot, take them to lunch, or pull them aside in the bathroom (assuming they're the same sex as you or you have one of those unisex facilities). Do whatever it takes to avoid going to your boss (or their supervisor).

Assuming you've tried that and still aren't getting the response you were hoping for, set up an appointment to meet with your boss. If you storm in immediately, you're bound to complain out of anger and frustration and may come across as being irrational, catty, or just bitchy. Setting up an appointment later in the day allows you to calm down and lets your boss know that you're not only serious about the complaint, but that you've taken some time to think about the problem and possible solutions. You do have possible solutions, right?

It's very important that when you walk into a meeting with a problem, you already have at least one solution to offer. Having multiple solutions will help you look even better. It's also vital that you let your boss know you've already taken measures to rectify the problem without involving a third party. Even though the attempt didn't work, it shows that you're not just eager to get someone in trouble with the boss.

Say, for example, that your problem is that the receptionist is screening your calls despite your frequent requests to have everyone put through to you. You've approached her twice after receiving complaints from callers that she continues to tell them you're "unavailable" when in fact you've been available.

Your possible solutions might be for your boss (who is also the receptionist's direct supervisor) to discuss the problem with her or for you to hire another assistant just for your calls. You may also discuss the possibility of getting a direct phone line to your office so as to bypass the receptionist entirely.

If you honestly can't think of one possible solution, don't afraid to say so to your boss. "I racked my brain over the weekend trying to come up with a viable solution to this problem. Unfortunately, I'm coming up blank and was hoping you'd be able to think of some ideas."

Just be prepared for solutions you might not like. Answering your own phone may not be realistic with your workload—and firing the receptionist might make you feel like a schmuck in the morning. Then again, she did refuse to put that call through from your blind date who needed to cancel Friday night. That was a very long wait at the restaurant before you phoned home to get your messages.

Did you know . . .

- The *Wall Street Journal* once estimated that 98 percent of all the papers on file in offices across the United States will never be looked at again.
- On an average U.S. Navy guided missile frigate, there are twenty tons of filing cabinets and paperwork. (**Source:** http://vigilanteventures .com/trivia/office.htm)

94

Faaaghet About It!

Blow off a bad day without going postal.

"The greater part of our happiness or misery depends on our dispositions and not on our circumstances."
—**Martha Washington**

Maybe you accidentally missed a big deadline and blew a huge account. Or spent nine hours substitute teaching a gaggle of fourth grade hooligans who kept launching spitwads at you. Maybe the party of six stiffed you after you waitressed your butt off, your hopes high for a gargantuan tip. Whether you're a six-bucks-an-hour janitor or a six-figure corporate raider, one thing's for sure—you're going to have a bad day at work once in a while.

So a few prepubescent punks or tightwad customers ruined your day—don't let them ruin your night! What you need is a strategy for blowing off a bad day at the workplace, a personalized routine or method to leave work crap at work rather than letting the stench of a rotten day waft in and stink up the fresh air of your personal time.

How, you ask? Easy—come up with a little routine for blowing off steam that's as individual as you are, giving your mind and body the signal, "Work's over. Now it's *me* time!" The trick is finding the thing that's going to be effective for you.

You jock-type chicks have it pretty easy when it comes to pegging your bad day blow-off activity—enjoyable exercise does the trick. A few laps on the treadmill, shooting hoops right after work, or contorting through a Pilates class all help move you from "aarrggghh" to " . . . aaah" just by working up a sweat. For those truly horrid days, consider throwing your swimsuit and towel in your gym bag and indulging in an after-workout sauna. Few furrowed brows can stay scrunched for long under direct extreme heat.

What if exercise bores you? Consider something soothing and spiritual to repair your frazzled nerves. Try some deep breathing while sitting in a dark room with some New Agey tunes playing in the background. Plenty of women swear by a hot bath as the key to unwind Utopia. Don't forget the candles, bath oils, and other froufrou stuff to turn your ordinary bath into a home spa. Or splurge on a foot massager—it feels great, and you never have to ask it to rub your feet or worry about your crusty heels and peeling pedicure!

Not sold yet? Get creative! Keep some crayons and a coloring book on your coffee table to recapture the kid in you. Or read a few pages of a saucy novel to get your mind off the work merry-go-round. Chant in your underwear as you visualize floating fluffy clouds. One caveat, though—make a conscious effort to keep it positive. Snarfing down a mixing-bowl-size serving of Chunky Monkey ice cream or pounding shots as you sing "One Bourbon, One Scotch, One Beer" may *sound* good, but you'll set yourself up for another dismal day as you lurch to work with a hangover, or too bloated to fit into your work uniform.

Chances are there'll be other crappy days in your future—learning to deal with it rather than letting it grind you down is one of the smartest moves you can make to manage your work attitude and stress level.

95

Tooting Your Own Horn

Angle for a promotion by showing you're worth it.

> "If women can sleep their way to the top, how come they aren't there? . . . There must be an epidemic of insomnia out there."
> —Ellen Goodman

If you were a man, this wouldn't even be an issue. You'd be so busy devising new ways to get noticed that you wouldn't be worried about hurting anyone's feelings or how it looks to your coworkers that you're angling for a promotion.

But you're not a man (OK, to be fair, let's say "some men"), and highlighting your assets and accomplishments doesn't come easy to you—although it should. You're a dynamic, professional woman, and if you don't stand up for yourself, who will? In order to move up the corporate ladder, you have to show off your portfolio.

If you really want to get promoted, set up an appointment with your boss to go over your accomplishments, current responsibilities, and aspirations within the company. Make it clear that you not only want a promotion, but deserve one. Be specific on what you're looking for in terms of money, title, and responsibilities, and then be prepared to put your money where your mouth is as to why you're qualified for the position.

You'll want to have all your ducks lined up: Who will take your current position? What have you done to bring in revenue for the company, or how have you cut costs? Mention any extra duties you've taken on, such as helping another department or writing articles to increase the company's exposure in the marketplace.

Don't be afraid to create a new position for yourself, if you can prove that it will really help the company. If you've taken classes that will help you in your new role, be sure to mention them—as well as your grade. "I've taken three night classes in marketing and received A-plusses in each of them" may help your plea.

Be careful not to put down anyone else in order to make yourself look better. In addition to looking catty, it could also get you in hot water later when that person becomes your boss. You're trying to move up in the company and get an expense account, not slide down the ladder to start cleaning toilets just to keep your job.

Keep in mind that not getting a promotion doesn't necessarily mean your boss doesn't think you deserve it. It could mean that the company doesn't have enough money right now or that there's no position open. Feel free to ask why you're getting passed over and ask for another evaluation in say, ninety days. You may feel pushy, but think of it more as perseverance. After all, that's certainly a quality your boss will appreciate—especially if you're convincing her that you're just the gal to land the big clients.

Fun Factoid

The average pencil will draw a line thirty-five miles long.

96

Throwing Out the Alarm Clock

Learn the secret to getting let go and liking it.

> "You can't be brave if you've only had
> wonderful things happen to you."
> **—Mary Tyler Moore**

The mood has been morose and your morale has been in the toilet, along with sales for the past quarter. The nasty rumors are true and one day you arrive to nothing but a sullen, stressed-out manager and a big fat pink slip. You've been let go!

Whether you're being laid off, fired, or simply forced out, your livelihood's not the only thing on the chopping block when the axe falls. Feeling forlorn, you can feel your self-esteem, reputation, and future shrivel in tandem with your paycheck. What's worse, you're not likely to get much notice before you're handed your walking papers. Strangely, even those of us who've been formally disciplined, scolded, or similarly spanked by the boss don't see it coming.

Believe it or not, there are a few empowering things you can do to help yourself after you're left to twist in the wind. If you feel you've been canned unfairly, be sure you grab the employee handbook or manual as you're cleaning out your cubicle. Look for written company policy on discipline procedures in the employee handbook, and scour it for clues that the company has to follow certain procedures (written warning, followed by disciplinary action, typically). If it hasn't, the handbook will give you clout in negotiating to get your job back.

Let's say you reluctantly admit your work performance has been less than stellar. Who'd have thought those three-hour lunches and napping on the job would come back to bite you! As much as it hurts, ask for the specific reason you're being let go, so you'll know what performance issues you must address. Asking puts you in a proactive, rather than reactive, stance, plus the answer may surprise you. No sense beating yourself up over what you suspect might be excessive absenteeism when sorry sales are the real cause.

The good news is, you'll most likely qualify for unemployment unless your conduct was deemed "grossly negligent." That should be reason enough *not* to karate chop your boss upon exit, or plant a farewell virus in the computer network, no matter how angry you are. If you've planned ahead and kept your résumé updated (note to self: update résumé), your job hunt need not skip a beat.

Whatever you do, do *not* react immediately and risk losing a good reference.

Don't say, "I quit" as a feeble attempt to save face. Quitting won't change the outcome and may discontinue any perks you have coming from being let go. Experts also tell you to avoid signing anything under duress.

Do consider this a golden opportunity. Feeling boohoo because you're unemployed? Consider this might be the universe giving you some impromptu downtime and a chance to evaluate your career. Maybe the powers that be saw you suffering along in support hose with a too-long commute and are giving you a chance to pursue your dream of owning a corner hot dog stand or starting a home school or kennel. Take time to reevaluate. Or get wild hair and take a six-week backpack trek through Nepal. Or volunteer to work in an orphanage in Guatemala.

Take a break from job hunting and spoil yourself occasionally. True, a $100 an hour massage and body wrap is probably not in Visa or MasterCard's best interest, but take time to exercise, meditate, and read a good book or two to recharge those batteries that job hunting will surely drain.

Speaking of funds, ease your mind by assessing the financial big picture. Will you be covering your butt with the healthy severance package? Are you a type A who's been stashing away cash for months? Are you a "pay Visa with MasterCard" kind of gal? Knowing how well-off (or in deep doo-doo) you are beforehand will spare you the nasty surprise of getting your debit card denied when you try to buy gas, or having to start selling blood plasma for grocery money.

And no matter how down you feel, remember: you were looking for a job when you found the last one!

ｽpeaking of ex-boｽｽeｽ ...

What are your past employers saying about you? Check myrefer ences.com or other reference checking services and find out for sure!

97

Time's Up!

Nip time wasters in the bud.

"Dost thou love life? Then do not squander time,
for that is the stuff life is made of."
—**Benjamin Franklin**

Saving time to squeeze out more leisure hours gets a big thumbs-up from any working girl. But what's the point of saving time at the office? you ask. After all, you have to stay until five o'clock anyway, so why knock yourself out?

Consider time saving a necessary and valuable skill at any job, allowing you to open up moments on your Day-Timer for brainstorming new business opportunities, hatching marketing schemes, and plotting long-term career plans—you know, all the work-related stuff that gets pushed to the back burner while you struggle to tackle daily tasks.

The key to discovering more free time is to root out and nip time wasting in the bud. Try these pointers for dealing with office windbags, marathon meetings, and other time-sucking distractions:

1. Some experts suggest keeping an official-looking red file or notebook on the corner of your desk. When a coworker dallies too long in your cubicle, stand up from your chair and reach for the red file—it's the body-language way to say, "You must go. I have urgent matters

tucked in this critical-looking folder that must be tackled immediately!"

2. When someone enters your office and asks, "Do you have a few minutes?" do not reply, "Sure, come on in!" Instead, say, "I have five minutes. What's up?" This communicates that you're accessible, yet have a limited amount of time. If an issue takes longer than a few minutes to discuss, suggest scheduling a meeting to cover it. Chances are, the party will prefer to give you the abridged version of his or her spiel, rather than postpone it until a meeting.

3. Have "do not disturb" time when you don't wish to be interrupted. Get an actual "Do Not Disturb" sign to put on your office door, or put your phone block on. If doing so feels grumpy to you, be silly with it by roping off the entrance to your cubicle with velvet rope, or donning a crazy hat you've dubbed the "don't bug me" hat. It sounds gruff, but your boss will likely appreciate your initiative, and you'll be setting a good example for lesser, lazier coworkers.

4. Take all seating except your desk chair out of your office. Anything office mates need to discuss can be said more quickly standing up. For most office chats, sitting is unnecessary and encourages taking a tangent into idle chatter—which you don't have time for. Can't take the chair out? Set a few files on the seat to discourage its use.

5. Jot down questions for your boss or coworkers, to ask all at one time. This is especially important if your boss is difficult to pin down. You'll be more efficient and will save time by not stopping midday to hunt for the person with the answer you need. Long-winded boss? E-mail your questions, rather than enduring a forty-five-minute face-to-face.

6. Keep to-do lists, important phone numbers, and other material in one single notebook—no more hunting for files and phone numbers endlessly.

7. Plan activities according to your energy level. Are you peppiest in the morning? Plan your toughest or most dreaded tasks when your

energy level is high first thing in the morning, and get them off your plate.

8. Check your voice mail three times per day, not several times per hour. Have your personal greeting help you by giving callers as much info as possible. For example, "We're open daily until 6:00 p.m. Check our website at xyz.com for more information." curtails a slew of "How late are you open? Where are you located?" time-sucking phone calls and call-back requests. And just because your phone is ringing doesn't mean you have to answer it. If you'd rather not be disturbed, let voice mail kick in (it's probably another "How late are you open?" call that your clever greeting will preempt anyway).

9. Make copies of common to-do or check-off lists for repetitive tasks. If your job is to back up computers and update the virus software in your department monthly, make a master copy of the check-off sheet, rather than saying every month, "OK, time to make a list of tasks for the computer backups . . ."

10. Group all errands together, and do them during your down energy time. Save prime times to work on important projects, not standing in line at the post office.

With all the extra time you'll have, maybe you can finally get around to cleaning out your old lunches from the break room refrigerator.

Some Office Workers Make Time to Nap

Factory workers and office personnel in China regularly take naps after lunch. According to Article 49 of the Chinese constitution, "the working population has a right to rest." Many Japanese companies provide employees with quiet, darkened relaxation rooms. (**Source:** http://vigilanteventures.com/trivia/office.htm)

98

Drowning in a Sea of Paper

Put a lid on excess paperwork.

> *"Less is more."*
> —**Ludwig Mies van der Rohe**

Seminar flyers. Unsolicited memos. Copies of old forms no longer used. If you think the junk mail you get at home is bad, try working with the in box some women have to deal with!

It's no secret that junk mail and excess paperwork are a strictly modern malady—not that we'd want to go back to the days of hand-lettered papyrus. Still, some in box–clogging correspondence can be positively annoying. You'd think with the proliferation of E-mail and PDF documents, the amount of paperwork handled would be cut way down. Not true: departments in many companies take to CC:ing all department members about the slightest policy update or most minor goings-on, in an effort to communicate with everyone.

If you're the kind of superorganized person who enjoys perusing any and every piece of material that crosses your desk, good for you. But for those of us whose time and patience is less than infinite, here are a few tips for putting a lid on excess paperwork.

First off, make it a policy to handle every piece of paper just once by dealing with each item as soon as you receive it. Let's say you get your incoming mail and find two memos, a class flyer, and an invitation to a coworker's lunchtime baby shower. Resist the urge to pile the memos until later ("No time to read right now . . . to the file pile they go!") by simply skimming the information. Are they minor FYI memos? Then simply read, remember, and toss. Memos that require action from you go directly into your "action items" folder to tackle later. The baby shower flyer gets tossed as you simultaneously write the date and time in your Day-Timer, and the class flyer gets shoved in your handy tickler or long-term folder, since it's so far away.

See how easy that was?

Here's another trick experts swear by: read the mail right next to the trash can or paper shredder, and read it standing up. Standing up discourages you from lingering over every little item too long, and tossing rather than saving unimportant items leaves less clutter for your desktop that'll just have to be dealt with later.

Of course, part of squelching unwanted paperwork is to get out of receiving it in the first place. Do you regularly receive catalogs and newsletters that you're not interested in reading? While you're standing next to everyone's mailbox, simply hand it off to the next person on the routing list, without even taking it back to your desk. Better yet, ask to be taken off the routing list altogether. If you regularly get carbon copied on memos that don't pertain to you, simply inform the memo author and ask to be taken off the list.

If you're lucky enough to have an assistant or a receptionist who performs duties for the whole team, ask her to weed out unwanted mail before she routes it to you. Just be explicit about the materials you want her to toss without your permission—telling her to toss all unsolicited magazines may have her "round filing" your long-awaited Spiegel catalog by accident!

Fun Factoid

In 1893, Chicago hired its first policewoman, Marie Owens. Chicago's female police officers were not allowed to wear uniforms until 1956. (**Source:** coolquiz.com)

99

Have a Nice Trip

Use these rules of thumb to survive a work-related trip.

"If the world were a logical place, men would ride side-saddle."
—**Rita Mae Brown**

Remember when going on a trip meant relaxing and having fun? Yes, those were the good old days—or at least the good old trips for pleasure. Now you're traveling for work and it's hard to imagine it not being the worst week of your life.

Well, chill out with the drama-making. Just because you're going to an insurance convention doesn't mean you can't enjoy yourself!

Your first rule of thumb is to set some ground rules. If you're going with any male coworkers, make sure you'll have separate rooms and that the company will be paying for your meals—not your coworker. Get your own company credit card or talk to the accountant about charging meals to your room, getting cash in advance, or at least getting reimbursed for whatever meals you pay for out-of-pocket.

Your next project is to do some research on the hotel and city where you'll be staying. Is there a pool? What's the weather like? Are there beaches or shopping nearby? A bookstore where you can go to browse and relax? Is there a nightlife? How safe is the city? Is there a bus route, or do you need to take taxis everywhere? What types of places would be of interest for a tourist? Is there a place to rent rollerblades or a moped near the hotel? Is there skiing, waterskiing, snowshoeing, or fishing nearby? The Internet should provide you with plenty of information. If not, call the hotel or the local Chamber of Commerce for the city and ask them to send you information. You may even want to ask the accountant if the company will pay for two rental cars if you're going on a longer trip with a coworker.

If your research leads you to believe that there's just too much to see and do on such a short trip, ask if the company will fly you in the night before—or the day after—the convention so you can sightsee or take in a show. If you've always wanted to see *Death of a Salesman* on Broadway but will miss it by one day, it may even be worth paying for your own hotel the extra night. New York is expensive, but living a ten-year dream is priceless!

Next, you'll want to pack as if you'll be stuck in a snowstorm for the entire trip. Bring plenty of good reading material, some crossword puzzle books, stationery or postcards and stamps, books on tape, or even your favorite movie. Bring a phone card in case you need to call someone and chat to get some sanity back in your life (without charging up the phone bill in your room). If you have busywork or something you can work on to get you ahead (so you can *really* take a vacation when you get home), bring it.

The most important thing to remember is that you get back what you put into the trip. If you go with a good attitude and a lot of preparedness, you're bound to have a good time.

Looking for a Good Excuse as to Why You Didn't Finish That Project?

Harold Ross, editor of *The New Yorker*, once asked writer Dorothy Parker why she had not yet written an article she had promised to produce. "Someone else was using the pencil," she answered.

100

You Talkin' to Me?

Decipher office body language.

"The body says what words cannot."
—**Martha Graham**

Winking, giggling, hair tossing, weak handshakes—each of these human behaviors says so much without uttering a word. Yet most of us go about our work lives blissfully unaware of how our movements might be giving information away.

Witness the power of body language! Experts suggest that the majority of human communication is nonverbal. Hard to believe a whole bunch of what we have to say is conveyed by head scratching, arm crossing, and brow furrowing. But understanding (and then manipulating) body language can work for you, plus tell you stuff about others that they're secretly fessing up to with their gestures.

Consider the all-important lean. Want to convey that you're qualified and up to the challenge during a job interview? Try leaning toward the interviewer. Leaning forward shows you have a point to make and conveys interest in the conversation: "Look, I'm so into what we're talking about that I have to lean in to tell you all about it!"

Conversely, leaning away shows some reservation in the discussion. It's as if the person is trying to put some distance between him- or herself and the information that is being offered. That's your clue to solicit comments from him or her, listening carefully for any "yes, buts" the person utters (which you'll promptly dispel, of course!). Remember how your dad would lean away in his chair at the dinner table when you asked if you could borrow the car? Case closed.

Conversation getting heated? Time to whip out the hand signals. Cops swear that making hand gestures that display open palms (i.e., holding your hands up and saying something comforting like "I understand") is a surefire way to defuse a heated situation. Use it with an open brow and soothing voice, rather than a scrunched-up brow, if you really want to bring it down a notch.

When it comes to the face, the eyes have it. Steady eye contact (not staring, though) is the universally understood way to impart interest in someone, or his or her conversation. Lack of eye contact is a no-brainer—lack of interest. Try this tip from employment author Martin Yate, described in his book *Resumes That Knock 'Em Dead*: to make eye contact look natural and steady without imparting a stalkerlike stare, move your eyes to a few points along a person's face—look in his or her eyes a few seconds, then look at the person's forehead, then his or her chin. Don't forget to glance down to check your notes or jot something down to seem less frozen.

Finally, the handshake is the body movement that can make or break a deal. Some women have a tendency to give a weak, spineless handshake, imparting the impression that they're frail and delicate. Don't be afraid to reach out and grasp that hand to convey confidence, but don't overcompensate with a bone-crushing handshake. Shake hands with a few friends or coworkers and ask them to critique your shake. It might seem silly, but a good handshake could give you the cutting edge over competition.

Need More Help?

Be sure to check out author Gordon Wainwright's book *Teach Yourself Body Language* for more body-language tips.

101

ʃaving Face

Regain your composure after you've lost your cool.

> *"Work has to include our deepest values and passions and feel-ings and commitments, or it's not work, it's just a job."*
> —**Matthew Fox**

D o you remember the "Walk of Shame"? The long journey back to your dorm room after a night of . . . whatever . . . that left you crashed out all the way across campus? Well, saving face at work after you've totally lost your cool makes the Walk of Shame look like a march up the escalator to heaven's gate.

There could be any number of reasons why you've gone off the deep end: a lost promotion, denial of a raise, or a stolen idea attrib-uted to the coworker who "just wanted to pick your brain." Whatever your rationale, losing your cool on the job is never a good idea. First, it makes you look out of control—which doesn't help your chances for management. Second, depending on the nature of your fit, it makes you seem childish. This is not to say that your argument isn't valid. On the contrary; it could be a righteous, albeit uphill battle that you're fighting. The point is, no matter how important your cause, you're likely to be *perceived* badly by anyone in yelling (or spitting) range.

So what can you do to regain your composure? Leave the room. This doesn't mean slamming doors and stomping out, it just means quietly walking away from the situation.

The next step is to return to the scene and apologize—not for being wrong, necessarily, but for becoming out of control. Your final step is to address your concerns in a normal speaking voice. Having notes to point out your concerns will help you look organized and like you took your "break" to pinpoint valid issues. Here's a sample run:

"I'm back. Sorry for the outburst, I guess I just feel very passionate about this issue. I've used the last five minutes to jot down some of my concerns. I think that it will help us all communicate to understand that there are two sides to this problem. I'd be interested in hearing your concerns as well."

Even if you get the cold shoulder or rolled eyes upon your return to the room, you can take pride in the fact that you've been able not only to calm down but also to think clearly enough to write down your concerns. Besides, it may have earned you some respect to break out of your comfort zone. Sitting in the corner and being a good little girl just isn't your style. And if everyone didn't know that before, they certainly do now.

Speaking of cleaning up your mistakes . . .

Did you know that Bette Nesmith Graham invented Liquid Paper? (At least she could admit when she made a mistake!)